"Life gives you many ingredients.
Which ones will you choose?"

WISH
SANDWICH

*A BLACK MAN'S JOURNEY FROM
GHETTO TO GLORY!*

BY JERRY B. BOWDEN

Wish Sandwich:
A Black Man's Journey From Ghetto To Glory!

Copyright © 2020 by Jerry B. Bowden

RHG Media Productions
25495 Southwick Drive #103
Hayward, CA 94544.

ISBN 978-0-578-79996-4 (paperback)

Visit us on line at www.YourPurposeDrivenPractice.com
Printed in the United States of America.

WHAT PEOPLE ARE SAYING

"Jerry B. Bowden is living proof of what a 'can do' attitude is able to overcome and achieve in life. His powerful story of transition from ghetto to glory is beyond inspirational for anyone wishing to experience their fullest potential, regardless of their circumstances."
   —Joel Weldon, Hall of Fame Professional Speaker

"Wish Sandwich will open your mind to the possibilities that surround you and begin to see your life from a new perspective."
   —September Dohrmann, CEO of CEO Space International

"It's not where you start, or even the journey along the way, but how you persevere and never give up on yourself."
   —Nathan DuPree, Pastor, Living Stones Church

"Readers will learn the transformative power of fully embracing and experiencing life even in hardships where golden nuggets called blessings are hidden."
   —Fabien W. Edjou, Life Coach | Author | Blogger

"A story of service, rebuilding and redesigning one's future, this saga will undoubtedly inspire others to aim higher."
   —Leigh Bursey, Author, Columnist, Housing Professional, Musician, Motivational Speaker, Formerly Homeless Youth

"Jerry's emergence from the depths of suppression and bondage is nothing short of inspiring. One cannot help but become transformed by this hero's journey."
   —Tesy Ward, Foundress and CEO of The Tesy Ward Organization

"*Wish Sandwich* is the epic story of Jerry Bowden's triumph in the face of overwhelming adversity."
   —Steve Bond, Lead Pastor, Summit Christian Church

"I was on the edge of my seat throughout the book, in suspense wondering how he was going to get out of a harrowing situation, or where his escapades would take him next."
   —Shiela Miller, Author, Memoirs of a Miracle Baby, A Testimony of God's Love

"This is a book that many men; especially African American men can relate to as it speaks to the daily struggles of life and how one can overcome them."
   —Pastor Warnell Brooks, MFT, Worship & Pastoral Care, The Bay Church

"*Wish Sandwich* is a compelling story of rising above your circumstances, using your God-given gifts and talents, and the opportunities life presents you to achieve what you desire."
   —Dr. Elizabeth Clamon, Founder of The Clamon Group, LLC, Award winning International Speaker and Author

"*Wish Sanwich* takes the reader through an impactful life story, probing and motivating the reader towards the realization that it is choices we make and not the circumstances we are dealt with that determine our success."
   —Dr. Kasthuri Henry, PhD, CTP. CEO, KasHenry Inc | #1 International Best-Selling Author | Professor (www.kashenry.com)

ACKNOWLEDGMENTS

First, I would like to thank my Lord and Savior, Jesus Christ, for giving me such an adventurous life full of experiences and richness that only comes through him.

I would like to extend to my beautiful wife, Michelle, my deepest, sincere appreciation and love for her support and hard work in helping to organize and edit the contents of this book. It was her inspiration and encouragement that led me to believe that I could become an author in the first place. We both believe my story and life experiences may be a source of inspiration and encouragement to young men trying to find their way in life.

I want to also thank my son and daughter for the many years we spent together in California. How you both overcame challenges and racial injustice to become top in your class and MVPs in your respected athletic fields, still inspires me today. I am so very proud of the adults you have become, and the way you are raising your own children. May God continue to be your source of enlightenment and purpose.

Life is like a "wish sandwich." It's what you choose to put into it that makes it satisfying, delicious, and nutritious.

TABLE OF CONTENTS

FOREWORD

by Michelle Calloway

I am delighted to see Jerry's life story finally come to light in his book, *Wish Sandwich*. I have known Jerry for 15 years now, and his stories have always fascinated me. The things he has experienced and survived from are unimaginable to most people. His stories need to be shared with the world.

Now that I have read this book, and have connected the dots between all the stories he has shared with me over the years, I am even more impressed by his resilient character, and his "can do" attitude.

Nothing seems to stop him. If he makes his mind up to do something, like this book, he figures out how, and doesn't stop until it's done. Then he's on to the next thing. He embraces the learning process and does not let the fear of failure stop him from taking on a project.

Throughout this book, *Wish Sandwich*, you will see that adversity, oppression, violence, and addiction did not keep Jerry from fighting hard for his dreams. Once he set his eyes on what a better life could look like, he did whatever he needed to do to get there.

I am honored to be a part of Jerry's story as he has impacted my life in ways that I am unable to describe with words. He is my best friend, my husband, my business partner, and a talented professional singer.

Even into his senior years of life, I have seen Jerry grow exponentially as a person, embracing his past mistakes, and choosing to improve upon himself daily. He is nearly blind now, yet that doesn't slow him down from expanding his mind and offering valuable insight in company matters. It is impressive to think of the commitment and persistence that it took for him to write this book when he can barely see. Thank goodness for modern technology and his willingness to figure it all out. True resilience!

I believe that the stories Jerry shares about overcoming adversity, with true grit and determination, will inspire many readers to push through, and not give up, no matter their current circumstances.

When we experience tough circumstances and obstacles in life, and we overcome them somehow, I believe we should share that wisdom with others, and not keep it to ourselves. Jerry has endured a lot, more than one human being should have to endure, but he rose above it all, and now is sharing his journey, life lessons he discovered, and how important the choices you make are.

He is opening up and exposing his vulnerabilities through these stories in hopes that they will impact you in a positive way. We all make mistakes, but the important thing to learn is that we can embrace them, learn from them, and move on toward better days. This book is Jerry's legacy, his gift to you.

May it help you see your life through a different lens, and inspire you to make good choices.

—Michelle Calloway, International Speaker, Author, and CEO, REVEALiO Software and Media Solutions (revealio.com), Tech With Heart Foundation (techwithheartfoundation.org)

INTRODUCTION

T his book is an exposé of my life's story starting from early childhood in New York City. Abuse, poverty, and abandonment led me to new worlds of opportunity and adventure. Joining the military during wartime helped me to escape teen homelessness and violence on the streets of Brooklyn. Being in an actual war zone strengthened my resilience and character, but it also turned my heart cold. Racial tensions were high within the ranks of the military. Drugs, music, and sex were my release, my escape.

Through the injustices and hard knocks that I have had to overcome in my life, I have equally been blessed with amazing opportunities that only come around once in a lifetime.

Every experience I include in this book is true and often unrestrained. My story may be synonymous to yours, in that you too have experienced hardship, grief, injustice, racial inequality, and discrimination. It took a lot of courage for me to disclose and write my truths on these pages, because they expose me, both personally and professionally. Hopefully, my vulnerability, and rawness will help you believe that **it IS possible to change your current situation, no matter how unimaginable that is for you right now.**

Some of these stories will make you smile, and some will touch your heart and spirit so deeply your eyes will water, and others will seem surreal and impossible. This is nonstop adventure at every turn of the page. **It is truly crazy that this is my life!**

I've had the pleasure of singing on stage with superstars like The Temptations and B.B. King. Women at my performances would swoon, and take their panties off, and throw them at me. Some women would come onto the stage, and engage me by thrusting and swaying their hips to the music. Men seemed to like my music too, because it created a fun, party-like atmosphere.

Throughout this book, I use the metaphor of a "wish sandwich." Have you ever had only two slices of bread, and wished you had some meat? I often experienced this scenario as a child. Being poor and hungry pushed me to want more. Beyond food, I craved more out of life.

The meat of life is an essential ingredient and takes on many forms. My stack looks this way, and yours will look different. In the end, you want your Wish Sandwich to be so scrumptious, full of vitality and nutrition, that you are rolling in satisfaction after completing it.

So, which choice will you make? Are you going to take those two empty slices of bread, and spend your life longing for what could go inside? Or, are you going to make the choice to go after what you want in life, and learn from those who have already figured out how to have an unlimited supply of meats? **Change your perspective, change your life!**

My story exemplifies, no matter how tumultuous life can be, you CAN overcome. God gives us the innate ability to rise above and succeed. As you will see in my story, God never abandons us, no matter the trials we face, he is there, and he will see us through. Just try him!

Poverty and a broken family life are typically a formula for failure, but not always the means to a tragic end. What changed everything for me was just the simple desire to want a better life. Education is paramount, and the catalyst that began the total transformation of my life. Knowledge is power. If only I had a mentor during my turbulent times, maybe I could have avoided many of my hardships.

Life is a never-ending learning process. I hope this book acts as a source of enlightenment about your current situation, and empowerment for where you know, in your gut, you want to go in life. If you do not know what you want in life, just follow the road to knowledge, because knowledge will lead you to your destiny.

Most of my life skills have been developed through trial and error, or what I like to call experiential learning. It hasn't been easy. I've had to work very hard for what I wanted. In the end, my journey has been very rewarding though, and I hope you find some meaning in it.

CHAPTER 1

Ghetto

My story begins as a poor black boy growing up in Brooklyn, New York. It was the toughest, roughest and meanest neighborhood in New York City. My parents had seven kids, and my dad worked as a local handyman.

Daddy grew up in the South. He was one of eight children, and he had worked as a picker in the tobacco and cotton fields since he was eight years old. Like many black children in those days, he had very minimal education. Farming was more important to the family economy than education, because it paid for food on the table and other essentials. My daddy had basic reading skills, and he knew how to count, especially his money. Although he only had a third or fourth-grade education, he was smart. He was street smart, and knew how to hustle and barter. He didn't trust people much and was very cynical.

He strongly believed that money was his only reliable friend. My daddy was a handsome, strong young man. He was six feet tall, light-skinned complexion, and had wavy black hair, that he combed back slick to lay flat against his scalp. He was quite the ladies' man.

Mama also grew up in the South. I do not know much about her childhood or background. I know she had a brother because I have met my uncle, but she also had a sister that I never met. My mother was a beautiful, brown-skinned black woman. She had a full head of shiny, black hair. She was absolutely stunning. Mama was smart too, and seemed more considerate, educated, and well-spoken than daddy.

When daddy and mama met in Goldsboro, North Carolina, they fell in love and relocated to Brooklyn, where they married and settled down together in the mid-1940s. Many black people left the South to seek a better life in industrialized cities like New York City, Chicago, Detroit, and other urban areas. These cities offered manufacturing job opportunities with good pay. Daddy taught himself many trades. He learned plumbing, concrete work, and interior painting. Mama stayed at home raising the kids.

Brooklyn is densely populated, and is one of five boroughs of New York City. It was a place where minorities and immigrants settled during the industrial revolution. In addition to good wages, Brooklyn provided affordable housing, public transportation, factory jobs, and easy access to the Financial District (Wall Street), in Manhattan. There were many segregated immigrant and minority communities in Brooklyn. For the most part, everyone got along as long as you respected the boundary lines of community and cultural taboos. In other words, stay amongst your own kind. It was a subtle kind of racial segregation. Workers were needed, and it didn't matter what color you were for certain jobs, but the kind of job and pay you got was selected based on your race and status.

Residential buildings were constructed of concrete, leaving no daylight between the buildings. These row houses were called brownstones. The landscape had some large maple trees lining the grassy areas adjacent to the street. Small neighborhood parks offered basketball courts, benches and tables surrounded with small plots of grass-covered areas. We called Brooklyn the concrete jungle due to its lack of greenery, and abundance of concrete surfaces and structures. There were two very large regional parks I remember, Prospect Park in Brooklyn, and Central Park in Manhattan. Prospect Park was the coolest park. You could run on grass forever. It had lots of little ponds and creeks with tadpoles, frogs and minnows that we boys use to catch in containers.

Being a product of intergenerational poverty, my family did not have a lot of money or economic prosperity. My relationship with other cultures was distant, or non-existent because I lived in a predominately black community. As a very young boy growing up in Brooklyn, I hardly ever saw a white kid. My parents and my community seemed to have heavily influenced me to dislike other cultures, especially white people.

Of course, at five years old, you have no idea what life is about or what challenges are ahead of you. You depend solely on your mother and father for everything, to protect, teach, feed, nurture, and love you.

All nine of us lived in a small apartment in Brownsville, Brooklyn, on Saint Marks Avenue. We had a wood and coal burning stove that heated the house, and provided a stove for cooking. I remember that stove so well because when mom and dad weren't around, my brothers and I played with fire and got burned a few times as a result.

We had a black and white TV, and we often enjoyed comedy shows like *Abbott and Costello*, *The Three Stooges*, *The Jack Benny Show*, a white comedy with a black butler named Rochester, and *Amos and Andy*, a black comedy show about two friends— one was ambitious, and the other one was lazy. My favorite out of all the shows was *The Little Rascals*, because those kids had some of the craziest and funniest adventures.

Music was a part of our home, whether it was being played over the radio, or family members singing, or watching performers play on television. I remember seeing James Brown, an up-and-coming black soul singer, who gave birth to "funk" music, on the *Ed Sullivan Show*. Boy, that man could dance! He had some signature moves that my brothers and I would try to copy because they were so cool.

One evening, when the family was watching the *Ed Sullivan Show*, this white guy started dancing while playing his guitar. My daddy exclaimed, "Hot damn! Look at that white boy go!" We thought it was so funny seeing a white man dance like a black man. We just laughed and laughed, because we had never seen a white man dance and sing like that before! That white man was Elvis Presley.

This chapter represents the first slice of bread, the foundation of my wish sandwich.

CHAPTER 2

Chaos and Violence

Mom and dad argued a lot, often getting physical, with dad slapping mom, or threatening to kill her with a knife. At five years old, I was terrified when they argued. I would cry, and yell at them to stop. I yelled, "Daddy, please stop! Don't hurt mama!" My sisters and brothers would be crying too, begging them to stop fighting. It got so bad, that my mama's brother, Uncle Bud, came over to try to talk to daddy, and they ended up fighting too. My daddy grabbed an axe, swung it at Uncle Bud, and missed. The momentum of the swing ended up cutting a gash in daddy's leg. I was horrified, and frightened at the amount of blood that was pouring out, and all the screaming that was going on. My older sister rushed in to help daddy with his leg. He ended up healing just fine, but that was a traumatic experience for me.

On occasion, mama would take me with her to the street market on Saint Marks Avenue. I loved going with mama because the merchants gave me fruit and candy. I remember one time when we went to the market, it hailed and mama protected me from the little ice balls by tucking me under a fruit stand awning until the downpour stopped.

On one of our visits to the market, mama visited this man who lived upstairs, above the store. Mama told me to sit on a wooden crate in the hall entrance and wait for her, as she disappeared with the man in the back room. The man was friendly to me, and he gave me candy while telling me to keep our visit a secret.

Mama ended up leaving daddy for this man, and she ended up leaving us boys too. Mama took my three sisters and left. I can recall having mixed feelings about it. I was glad the fighting was over, but I was sad that my mama and sisters were gone.

In those days, it was common for a woman entering a new relationship to abandon her boys, out of fear that the man in the new relationship would resent the boys, and see them as a threat, leading to potential abuse. The girls, however, were seen as non-threatening, and accommodating to the new relationship.

My daddy was very bitter, because mama left him and abandoned her boys for another man. He was angry and unforgiving. He would always bring her up when scolding us, saying, "You are just like your no-good mammy!" Maybe that is why he would beat us so mercilessly. Daddy hated mama for her betrayal, and he hated the idea that mama's boyfriend would be raising his daughters. To him, it was a major insult added to injury. This man took his wife, and daddy feared he would also abuse his daughters.

Mama, in her new relationship, had seven more kids. My seven brothers and sister did not grow up around us, so we were not close. As with many broken relationships, there are unintended consequences to the children. I don't think either of my parents knew the lifelong impact their separation could cause their children.

After my parents separated, my dad got us a dog, and got himself a girlfriend. He had lots of girlfriends, and loved to drink and dance. The dog was a boxer breed and not very well trained, but he was fun to play with. Daddy took us boys to Coney Island, an amusement park on the shore of the Atlantic Ocean. When we returned home, the dog had gotten onto the stove and ate our dinner. My daddy beat him just like he would beat us when he got angry. I felt so sorry for the dog, because he was hungry most of the time, just like us.

We didn't have much money, but daddy seemed to be doing his best to provide a good life for his boys. He took us to Coney Island a lot, and we mostly played in the sand under the Boardwalk, and in the ocean. Daddy would always manage to find enough money to buy us hot dogs at the "World Famous Nathan's Hot Dogs" stand. They were so delicious! Sometimes he would even buy us cotton candy.

Daddy bought himself a 1954 canary yellow Oldsmobile 88. We really loved that car. He would take us joy riding, and sometimes treat us to White Castle hamburgers, where you could order a dozen bite-sized burgers for 25 cents each. My brothers and I tore those burgers up! We enjoyed these times with daddy, and for a while, everything seemed like it was going to work out alright.

One summer day, daddy said he wanted to take us boys for a joy ride. We all jumped in the car and drove to the country, and stopped at a farm on Long Island, New York. He ended up leaving us there.

Yep, he just got in his car and drove off. We didn't know what was happening. We didn't know these people on the farm. All I could do was cry and scream, "Daddy, don't go! Daddy, come back! Daddy! Daddy!" It was a devastating day. My two older brothers and I were in complete shock. Pete was only two years old, so he didn't have much of a reaction. Us older boys knew what it felt like to be abandoned by a parent, but this was absolutely life-crushing.

Mama was gone, and now daddy was gone too.

The farm people he left us with were mean and abusive, both physically and emotionally. We had to get up early, work hard all day, and go to bed early. No television watching either. My chore was to feed the hogs the "slop." What an awful smell! It stunk like nobody's business.

I didn't like it there, and I didn't want to be there. I was very sad. I would often cry myself to sleep. My older brothers were sad too. Bubby, who was 12 years old, did his best to be strong as the oldest brother, but I could tell he was hurting as well. Several weeks passed.

One night while in bed, I heard my daddy's voice in the other room. He was cussing at the farm people for some reason. He came into our room and told us to get our clothes on. "I'm taking you with me." He said, as he pulled back our covers. We were so happy! We got in the car so fast, hoping he would not change his mind.

Daddy was sharply dressed when he came to take us home with him that night. He had on a camel-hair, cashmere, long overcoat, color-matching trousers, hat, and brown wingtip shoes. He was our handsome rescuer. It is puzzling how I remember these details, but I do. I was six going on seven years old. He drove us away in his canary yellow Olds 88. I didn't understand any of what was going on, but was glad to be away from those farm people.

Daddy moved us into a small brownstone apartment at 31 Hart Street, in the Bedford Stuyvesant neighborhood in Brooklyn. Our block was between Marcy Avenue and Nostrum Avenue. It was conveniently located near the P.S. 54 elementary school we attended. We had been on the farm for about one month before moving to 31 Hart Street.

I remember the first day of school. I was following a group of kids out of the back door after school let out. I wasn't familiar with the neighborhood yet, and I followed the kids thinking it was the way home, but I ended up getting lost in the Marcy projects. I found myself surrounded by high-rise buildings, overhead trains with shadowed busy streets, people loitering, and people yelling at each other in nearby apartments. The projects are where low-income people and gang members lived. I walked around tearfully lost and frightened, when a white man from my block recognized me and took me home. It was a scary experience in a very rough neighborhood, and I made sure to never go back there again.

Our apartment on Hart Street had one bedroom, one bathroom and a kitchen. The entrance to the apartment was located in the living room where we slept and played. There was a small hallway separating my dad's bedroom from us.

The bathroom was located within the small hallway, and the kitchen was adjacent to where we slept in the living room.

My three brothers and I slept in the same double-sized bed. It wasn't very clean. I had a bed wetting problem, and we had no clean sheets. Sometimes we slept on the mattress with only a blanket to cover us.

Gigantic bed bugs would feast on us, so we did our best to get rid of them. We would set a paper roll on fire and run it along the seams of the mattress where the bed bugs hid to burn and kill them. They were so big that you could hear them pop when you squeezed them. We never were able to totally get rid of them, so we had no choice but to share our bed with these biting blood-suckers.

A man was shot dead on the property next door, in the backyard near to where we slept. They left his body in the yard for a couple of nights. We were young and scared. One night, while all four of us were falling asleep, the shade flew up on the window, exposing the dead body on the ground. Two of my brothers flew under the bed, while Pete and I lay shivering from fear under the covers. It was funny because our imaginations ran wild, causing us freak out when the shade suddenly flew up. Our dad teased us that we were scaredy-cats for hiding under the covers and under the bed. We laughed for a long time after that. My daddy always reminded us of that time.

We loved sweet foods like Kool-Aid, and sweet potato pudding, mashed sweet potatoes, and cinnamon and butter. Once, daddy came home with what we thought was sweet potatoes for our favorite dish. It was orange in color like sweet potatoes. We asked daddy to pile it on our plates, as the four of us sat around the kitchen table. We all dug in and our facial expressions said the rest. "Ooh, that's not sweet potato pudding!" we cried, wincing. Turns out, it was wild rutabaga roots my dad had scavenged from the yard. My daddy replied, "You better eat every goddamn bit of it, or I'm going to beat the shit out of you." We all began to cry because we knew we were going to get beaten.

Whenever my dad wanted to punish us, it usually included a beating, and restricting us to sit on the trunk in the small hallway of our apartment for hours. So, my brother Butch and I would rip blank pages from the books that daddy kept in his curio nearby, and we would have a picture drawing contest. Butch was by far the better artist. My daddy caught us tearing blank pages from his books, and we got a whipping for that too.

My daddy worked every day, leaving us home alone. My older brother Bubby was left in charge. That didn't work too well because Bubby had his priorities, and that did not include watching over his brothers. He had his own social life to manage, and most of the time he left us to fend for ourselves. Even though I was the third youngest, my daddy would often put me in charge, because he felt I was smarter than my other brothers. That didn't go over too well either. My brother Butch and I fought fierce battles, and the landlord who lived below us would tell my daddy when he came home about our fights. I heard him tell my daddy that he shouldn't leave us alone, because he thought we were going to kill one another.

Butch and I were very close in age, and our birthdays were only three days apart. Oftentimes, we would have to share gifts together, and we always had to celebrate our birthdays at the same time.

One Christmas, we got a bike that we had to share together. That didn't work out well at all! Our fighting worsened over who was going to get to use the bike. So, Butch went out and stole a bike from somewhere in the neighborhood. He brought it home, and daddy asked him how he got the bike. Butch admitted he took it, and daddy beat him. I was told to take the bike back. So, I rode the bike around the neighborhood for a while, and then returned home. I told my daddy they said we could keep the bike (a little white lie never hurt anybody). Now, Butch and I had separate bikes, but we still argued and fought.

My oldest brother Bubby spent most of his time hanging out on the block with his friends. He was a really good singer. He was part of a group called "Take Five." That group went on to be famous, without Bubby. Doo-wop style music was the happening thing in the 50s. Butch and I started our own group called "Little Butchie and The Bops." This is when I discovered my God-given talent. I could really sing!

I was such a daredevil, never thinking about consequences. I taught myself how to ride a bike, and nearly amputated my finger when I crashed into a parked car's headlight. We were having a rock fight, throwing rocks at each other. I was taking cover behind a tree when a big rock sailed by me. I stuck my head out from behind the tree to tell the kid not to throw big rocks like that, because you could really hurt someone, and caught a big rock with my forehead, requiring stitches. Unfortunately, violence and hostility were an environmental phenomenon living in Brooklyn.

We used to play roly poly, a baseball game that would facilitate how you rotated batters. You'd hit the ball, someone would try to field it, and depending on how far you hit it, the fielder could relay the ball to the closest fielder to the batter. The fielder would roll the ball to hit your bat. As the batter, you would have to lay the bat on the ground horizontally. If the rolled ball hit your bat and popped up, you, the batter, had to catch it before it hit the ground. If you missed it and it hit the ground, or if it hit your bat and it didn't pop up for you to catch it, you were out and the original ball retriever was up at bat. The other way you could be out was if the ball was caught on the fly. Then there was also fast ball. It's like baseball but the strike zone was a square drawn on the wall behind the batter. If the ball hit inside the square, or if the batter missed it on the swing, it was a strike. The cool thing is you didn't need a catcher, because the ball would bounce off the wall right back to the pitcher.

My daddy worked a lot, but we still struggled with money. I recall often eating mayonnaise and onion sandwiches because that was all I could find after scavenging the kitchen for anything to eat. My daddy drank a lot of booze, and when he got drunk, he'd beat us with anything he could get his hands on. He would always threaten to kill us, saying we would be better off dead.

He couldn't keep a girlfriend; he would get drunk and beat them too. I remember one of his girlfriends tried to jump out the second story window. My daddy grabbed her in the nick of time. His girlfriends were very nice to us and we grew to like them, but he would end up beating them and they would leave him. I guess he blamed us for his failures and problems. All but one of us boys looked a lot like mama, and the one that didn't was his favorite, Pete. When daddy would go on his drunken rampage, he would tell us, "You are just like your no-good mammy!"

I was very afraid of my daddy. He would beat me so badly that I would pee on myself, and then he would beat me some more for peeing on myself. Seventy years later, the abuse still brings tears to my eyes. I was so afraid of him. When I was eight years old, I decided to run away from home and go to Coney Island Amusement Park. I figured I could sleep under the boardwalk and beg for food. So, my friend and I sneaked on the GG train bound for Coney Island. After hanging out at Coney Island for the day, we decided to take the train back to the neighborhood, because my friend had to go home. It was getting late, so I thought I would just sleep in the neighbor's yard under the shrubs for the night.

My daddy had been riding in his friend's car, canvassing the neighborhood looking for me, when he spotted me entering the neighbor's yard. He grabbed me and I started crying because I knew he was going to beat me. I said, "Daddy please don't beat me," as he forced me into the car.

My daddy's friend tried to talk my daddy out of beating me, but to no avail. When he got me upstairs in the apartment, he grabbed a utility cord, put my head between his legs, pulled my pants down, and began whipping me. All I could do was run in place with my head held tightly between his legs, as I tried to escape the pain that came with each lashing. He beat me so bad that I peed on myself.

It seemed like the more daddy beat me, the more defiant and reckless I became. I would cut school with my friends to explore Brooklyn. We used to hitch a ride on the back bumper of public buses, barely able to hold on at speeds of 30-40 miles per hour.

I would often ride the bus to the pool. I loved swimming and diving, even though I only knew how to doggy paddle. I decided to jump off the sixteen-foot high diving board. I found out very quickly after plummeting to the bottom of the pool, just how deep it really was. It seemed like it took forever for me to reach the surface, and I began to panic that I would run out of air. I finally broke the surface, gasping for air.

This chapter represents the horseradish I would put on my bread to add hot, spicy flavoring to my wish sandwich.

CHAPTER 3

Children's Center

D addy was inside the office talking with social workers at the Children's Center in Manhattan, while my brothers and I played with toys in the waiting room. Daddy came out of the office and told us we were going to have to stay there, because he "couldn't take care of us no more."

I immediately jumped to my feet, while reaching for him, crying out, "Daddy, don't leave us! Daddy, please! Daddy, don't!" My brothers were crying out too. We were all astonished that this was happening to us again. I was eight years old.

The social workers came out of the office and tried to console us boys. They then took us to our dormitories where we would be housed for the duration of our stay. Each of us were evaluated mentally, socially, and medically to determine our therapy plan and social placement within the Children's Center community.

I remember meeting with a psychiatrist, and looking at some flash cards that looked like butterflies. I had many meetings with the psychiatrist. There was a period of time that I couldn't actually walk because of these strange knots that covered my legs from the ankles up. It was the strangest phenomenon that the doctors couldn't explain. It lasted for two weeks, and then I was up and running again as if nothing ever happened.

I made new friends fairly easy, and began to explore my new community close to Central Park, which is a regional park in the center of Manhattan, New York. It was so large you can get lost in it like in a forest, except, you're in the middle of a city.

I was just a kid, and a resilient one at that. If there was intrigue and adventure, nothing was going to hold me down from having fun. I loved life. I loved to explore Central Park, eat Chinese apples (pomegranates), hot dogs, and knish. I am not sure how they got the name Chinese apples, but that is what we called them. I used to buy lemons to suck on because I was told they are good for your singing voice. Sucking the lemons made me feel cool like a singer, and I loved music.

One day my dad came to visit us at the Children's Center, and I thought he was going to take us home with him. Nope. He did take my youngest brother Pete, though. He was four years old. Pete was always daddy's favorite. He left us older boys, and for the most part we were okay with it. We had adjusted pretty well to our new life, and we were with people who cared for us. We felt safe.

Woodycrest Children's Home

We stayed in the Children's Center for a little over a year until it was established where our long-term care would be provided. They loaded us brothers into a van and told us we were going to live at a children's home called Woodycrest.

When we arrived at Woodycrest, I realized it was a converted mansion. It was located at 161st Street and Jerome Avenue, Bronx, New York, near Yankee Stadium. The primary building was made of brick and was four stories tall. The second building, across an open courtyard, was where the gym, swimming pool and Robert's Hall dormitory was located. The entire site encompassed five city blocks on a hillside.

Woodycrest was a privately-operated boarding home for troubled and abandoned children. It was segregated by gender and age. There were the Cowboys for ages 7-9, where I was placed. My live-in counselor was Mr. Carter. My brother Butch was placed in Duryea, (Dur-ree-ay), for ages 10-13, and his live-in counselor was Mr. Durant. My brother Bubby was placed in Taft, for ages 14-16, and his live-in counselor was Mr. Craft. The oldest group before exiting the home, was Robert's Hall, for ages 17-18.

There was a single girl dormitory for ages 12-18. One of the windows in the Cowboy dormitory had a view of the girl's shower. Being young curious boys, we would occasionally sneak a peek. The girls knew we would watch sometimes, and it seemed as though they didn't mind us looking. One of the girls, named Barbara, had the biggest breasts. They shot straight out and would command our attention. She often came to the window while lifting her arms above her head, and would just stand there, giving us a glorious show. The counselors later found out, and put up curtains and blinds.

I had a crush on a very beautiful counselor named Veronica. She was probably in her twenties, and I was nine and in love with her. She knew I loved her, and she would just smile and treat me so nice. She had long, dark brown hair, olive-colored skin, and a face so beautiful. At Woodycrest, people were always coming and going, so you could always expect change. I remember the day that I found out that Veronica was leaving Woodycrest. I cried as I said goodbye to her. She gave me the most endearing hug and she left. My heart soon mended, and I was back to being a wild and mischievous boy.

Elementary school-aged kids had class on-site, and the older kids went to a public school off-site. Miss Archer was my 3rd and 4th grade teacher. She was an older Caucasian lady with silver gray hair. I really loved Miss Archer. She loved me too, especially my penmanship. She used to always compliment me on my perfect lettering. She also complimented me on my math skills, and my ability to master multiplication and fractions. She was a wonderful teacher and friend. I loved her and will never forget the impact she had on me.

I graduated to the 5th grade class. Miss Poisenheim was another wonderful Caucasian teacher that I loved. Besides just teaching us the basics, she also spent time teaching us about life in general. She would turn on the television every afternoon after our classroom lessons, and would let us watch the Loretta Young Show. It was like watching a live drama show. Watching that show exposed us to real life events that she hoped would shape our character and personal development.

Mr. Carter, my counselor, was a military-style disciplinarian. He would make sure we made our beds tight and maintained good hygiene. Even though I was now nine years old, I still had a problem with urinating in the bed during sleep, and he was pretty hard on me for it. He would embarrass me in front of the other kids. They would make jokes, and call me names like, "The Midnight Sailor," or say things like, "Sniff, sniff I smell a sailor." I was so ashamed and humiliated, I tried to hide it by pulling the covers up on my bed, even with the wet sheets. Mr. Carter caught me doing that and stripped my bed, and then rubbed my face in the sheets.

I started fighting anyone who made fun of me. I didn't like being made fun of for something that I couldn't seem to control. I recall feeling so depressed that I said to myself I would stop talking to people and just withdraw. That only lasted a day. I would always break out of my withdrawn state by my overwhelming need to play with the other kids, and that always made me happy.

Some of the cool activities at Woodycrest were arts and crafts, theater, Friday night dances, gym, and swimming. I also learned boxing and rope climbing, and enjoyed playing basketball and volleyball. I was a husky kid, but very athletic.

One time we were playing sandlot football with my friends. They used to run really fast to avoid me from catching up to them. The ball carrier I was pursuing had blockers around him. I was big and could run fast for my size. I hit the blockers into the ball carrier and knocked them all down to the ground. It was fun and I felt so awesome.

We had a chapel where we held our theatrical plays and weekly worship services. I always sat with my friends during worship service, and we'd be singing hymns like, "The Old Rugged Cross," "Holy, Holy, Holy," "In the Garden," etc. Every hymn ended with us singing, "Amen." The black kids took that as an opportunity to harmonize and hold the "Amen." It sounded so beautiful, but Mr. Ingles, our administrator, would say, "Now, now, boys!" He was what we called a "white man with no rhythm." We kept harmonizing anyway, and he would keep trying to quiet us down. We loved harmonizing and got pretty good at making hymns more soulful.

I was very good in the arts. I was in several plays, where I received lots of laughs and ovations for my performance. One time, I wore a blonde wig to play a girl in a skit called, "Has Anybody Seen My Girl?" The song lyrics were about a white girl, five-foot-two inches tall, with blue eyes. And, there I was strutting across the stage in a flapper dress and heels, five-foot nine inches tall, black with brown eyes. I got lots of whistles and laughs. I loved performing, and always looked forward to my next opportunity to dawn the stage.

I learned to read sheet music and play the piano. My music teacher, Mr. Green, said I had a natural talent. He identified that I played by ear rather than by reading the music, and would tell me to knock it off, and practice reading the notes more. The boys I played with knew that Mr. Green was gay and wore a toupee, and they made fun of him. He didn't like that I hung out with these boys, and that I loved to play sports more than practice piano, so he dropped my lessons. How unfortunate, because having the talent to play an instrument to accompany my singing talent would have been phenomenal.

I had so many wonderful experiences at Woodycrest that were life-changing. They helped mold me into who I am today. Woodycrest helped me start the process of rehabilitation, by providing me with a stable environment, education, culture, and community. Although these experiences were important and instrumental, this was just one of many developments I needed to get me on the right path in life.

Bear Mountain

Every summer, we would spend three months up in Bear Mountain, New York, at Woodycrest Camp. This was a phenomenal campground along the shores of Lake Cohasset. We had canoes, row boats, and our own swimming area. Each age group had their own sleeping cabins and shared multiple out-buildings for showers and toilets. We had an open-air central dining room that also served as a recreation room. Below the dining room was a mini store where we could buy candy bars. My favorite candy was Almond Joy and PayDay. I loved candy! Cookies and cake too!

It was the most beautiful setting with big shade trees and tall pine trees scattered throughout. I had no fear, so I would climb to the top of these fifty-foot trees. In the morning we would wake up at 6:00 a.m. to bugle call, which sounded something like, "It's time to get up, it's time to get up, it's time to get up this morning."

We got up, washed our face, and brushed our teeth, made our beds, and cleaned up the cabin. Then the trumpeter would blow the "Charge" song repeatedly until everyone was in formation. We would charge down the dirt and rock-laden hill from the cabin as fast as we could. It was so much fun for us nine and ten-year-olds, jumping from rock to rock. I was the second fastest boy in my cabin next to "Froggy," a nickname we gave Ernest Robinson because his feet pointed outward like a frog.

We would pledge allegiance to the flag as it was being raised to the top of the pole. Afterwards, we would take our seats in the large dining hall to have breakfast, and then the camp supervisor would announce the daily schedule of events. We sang songs after breakfast before being dismissed.

We would then clean outside the cabin, rake the ground clear of any new debris, and clean the toilets. Then the activities would start. We would go boating, canoeing or swimming in beautiful Lake Cohasset. Some of us would take the lifeguard test and learn other safety skills related to boating and canoeing. Some of the lifeguard training required you to be able to jump in the water without submerging, and swim with a drowning victim. We learned CPR and how to resuscitate a drowning victim. We had to swim a certain number of laps to get certified.

We used to compete in canoe regatta racing. We raced against other camps in the Bear Mountain area. Our camp was predominately inner-city black kids, who happen to be very athletic. Our canoe racing team consisted of four young black boys; 13-15 years old. We won first place every year and were the team to beat. Our team used coordinated, precision paddling strokes, which made our canoe sail through the lake water faster and straighter to the finish line. Our canoe was made of fiberglass, which was lighter and faster than the wooden canoes. Our canoe stood out from the rest. It was the only white canoe with four black boys manning it. At the end of a race we would hold our paddles straight up close to our shoulders like a soldier's salute. One time another canoe collided into us and turned our canoe over. But, because of our lifeguard training, we knew how to shake the water out of a submerging canoe and climb back in. What an awesome experience at Woodycrest, something I would have never gotten growing up in Brooklyn.

Another competitive activity we did while at summer camp was playing softball. That was so much fun, because we would always see who could hit the most home runs over the fence, and who could hit the ball the farthest. Froggy could really belt the ball far. He was a heck of an athlete. There was also Juan, and Dallas. These boys were on our canoe racing team, softball, basketball and football teams. I was always stocky, but very athletic and could run. I was playing catcher, and this kid was coming around third base, heading to home plate when the ball was thrown to me for the tag out. Not only did I tag him out but I also laid him out. The crowd in the stands went wild.

Hiking was another fun activity we did once a week. We would call them nature hunts. We would take 26-mile hikes through the forest. This forest was very unique. Its thick tree canopy with rays of sunlight shining through made it seem mystical. The forest was damp and there was a lot of moss on the rocks and fallen logs. We saw salamanders, black racers, copperheads, rattlers, and many other species of snakes and turtles.

There were box turtles and snapping turtles, flying squirrels, and lots of species of frogs. I would capture these critters with my bare hands. One time while on a hike, I reached into a pond and grabbed a very colorful snake. As I lifted the snake out of the water it bit me on my finger. I reacted by throwing the snake up in the air. It came down on Dallas, who was terrified of snakes. He did a shimmy and dance that made everyone laugh. I was telling Dallas to grab the snake before it gets back into the water, but to no avail. It escaped. So, my finger had two puncture wounds from the snake bite. The activity counselor thought it might be venomous, so he called the State Trooper and I got to ride to the hospital with sirens blaring. I thought that was pretty cool. It turned out it was non-venomous.

My friends and I discovered an old silver mine on one of our hikes. It looked mysterious, so we got on our bellies and crawled in to see what it was like inside. The cavern openings were so small that an adult body could barely fit, but we were curious, so we pressed on. It was pitch-black, and the only one that had a flashlight was my friend John, in the front of our single file line. There was no room to turn around, and the further we went in, the more anxious I felt.

Twenty minutes of crawling felt like a year, when we finally came to a vast opening in the cave that encompassed a murky pond in the center. Whew! I was so relieved to stand upright and take a deep breath! We all hollered and cheered as our voices echoed off the cave walls. What an adventure that turned out to be!

We used to play tricks on each other all the time. I played a trick on my friend, François. He was from France and we played together a lot. We were playing with a soccer ball, and I knew that there was a yellow jacket's nest in the bushes near where we were playing. I kicked the ball over into the nest and François went to retrieve it. The yellow jackets were pretty pissed off and they let François know it. I was laughing at first, but he started running toward me and the yellow jackets were in pursuit. They were stinging both of us as we were running. We were booking it! We ran and laughed so hard. He said he would get me back. I said, "In a way you already have, because I was stung too!" Woodycrest always held yearly award events at the campground. There were chess tournaments, archery tournaments, boxing tournaments and the biggest fish-catching tournament.

This one particular year, I was fishing in a rowboat by myself when I felt a big pull on my line. It almost yanked my pole right out of my hands. I started screaming, "Help! I've got a whopper here!" I pulled and reeled the line as hard as I could to bring the fish in without tipping my boat, or losing the fish. As the fish got closer to the boat, I could see how big it was, and it was putting up a real good fight. I did it though. I got it in the boat and stood up to show everyone who was cheering me on from their boats.

The fish turned out to be a five-pound large-mouth bass. The camp director announced me as the winner that night at dinner. In celebration, the camp chef prepared the fish so that I and my best buddies could feast on it. I felt like a champion! It was an awesome feeling.

I also learned archery and arts and crafts. We used to make papier-mâché puppets and lanyards using various stitches like diamond, box, and cobra stitch. We had theatrical plays where every group participated by directing their own skit.

There was competitive boxing as well. This one kid, Ronald Prendergast, and I were matched together for just about every physical competition. Our bodies were built similarly, and we weighed about the same for fat kids. He was my white twin brother, so to speak. We would have sprint races between us and, of course, we were always paired up for boxing matches.

Ronnie and I had fierce matches because we were both very competitive, and neither wanted to lose to the other. I won one boxing match where I gave him a bloody nose. He won one boxing match where he gave me a busted lip. These boxing competitions made me a good fighter. After everything was all said and done, Ronnie and I were still friends. I went to summer camp the entire stay at Woodycrest, about six years. It was an experience of a lifetime in which I would have never gotten raised in Brooklyn with my parents. In fact, 99% of children don't get to experience the beautiful childhood given to me by Woodycrest Children's Home. Just one of my many blessings.

Bullies

In the fall, school started up again, and I got into a fight with this big white kid in shop class. He was bullying me, and I was intimidated by his size. We had an argument, and he punched me in the face, so I hit him with a hammer that was on the table next to me. The shop teacher stopped the fight and the kid said he would get me after school. The kids at the school were anticipating the fight, and were planning to watch. At the end of the school day, all my friends were egging me on to kick his ass, but to be truthful, I was apprehensive. I waited for the kid to show up to fight, but he didn't show up. I can't remember exactly why, but I was okay with it.

Another time, I was being bullied by this black kid from school as I was walking home to Woodycrest with my friends. This kid started picking a fight with me in front of the drug store with a crowd of on-lookers. I got into my boxing stance, bobbed and weaved, and hit him with a right hook so hard that it broke his jaw. He instantly grabbed his jaw and the fight was over. The drug store owner called the cops and they made us disperse and go home. The kid's friends tried to instigate him into another fight with me, but I always won, so he finally stopped trying. Growing up in Brooklyn is rough, and you have to know how to fight to defend yourself or the bullies will punk you relentlessly.

My daddy would come around every now and then to visit us boys, but I found his visits more annoying than they were comforting. It became apparent to me how ignorant daddy was, and it made me feel embarrassed to have him around.

While in the Duryea group, for 10-14-year-olds, I was still having a bed-wetting problem. The counselors were frustrated and determined that my bed-wetting was a result of laziness. Even though they tried to cure me using many methods, none worked. They would wake me in the middle of the night to use the bathroom, but I would still end up wetting the bed. They decided to get me a rubber mattress. I was so embarrassed and was often depressed.

One morning after wetting the bed, Mr. Durant told me in an angry tone to take the soiled sheets down to the laundry room in the basement. Our dormitory was located on the third floor and I needed to take the sheets down the stairs to the basement. The stairwell was rectangular with a large opening in the middle. If you looked over the banister, you could see all the way down to the basement level. Being an adventurous boy, I would often slide down the banister rather than walking down the stairs. Well, this day the unimaginable happened. As I was sliding down the banister with the soiled sheets, I lost my balance and slipped over the railing into the abyss.

At first as I was spinning in the fall, I was in shock, not understanding what was happening. As I regained consciousness, I was lying in a pool of blood on the first-floor landing of the stairway. By the grace of God, I hit a steel column on the way down that broke my fall. The steel post gashed open a wound on my right-side chest area and my right thigh in two places. I yelled for help, and when they found me they rushed me to the hospital. They stitched me up good, and told me to rest, and take it easy.

My daddy was notified, and he came to the hospital. Once he found out that I was going to be okay, he threatened to beat me for being so stupid and careless. He was so angry, that the hospital staff had to calm him down.

I know that I was lucky to be alive. I could have easily hit my head or been crushed by falling from multiple stories, but that didn't happen. God was looking after me. I had a few more close calls, like the time I was sleigh riding and ran into a car, and another time I wrapped myself around a tree. Some say I had a death wish, but I was just adventurous.

Woodycrest Avenue is a one-way street with a steep 30% slope. Some of us boys would roller skate down the hill because we could pick up some serious speed. The challenge was to maintain control while going so fast, because at the bottom of the hill was a heavily trafficked intersection. If we lost control, we would skate right into traffic. We would strap metal skates to our sneakers at the top of the hill, get into a crouched position, and blaze down the hill. We would gain so much speed that sparks flew from the metal wheels. It was a ton of fun and luckily, I never got hurt. Unfortunately, not all of my friends came away unscathed.

Woodycrest was an awesome place to grow up. Part of Woodycrest overlooked Jerome Avenue and we could see Yankee Stadium and Babe Ruth Field, which is now the newly built home of the Yankee Stadium. As a teenager, I became even more rowdy and rambunctious. I used to go to the after-school grind parties. That is where the lights are low and the guys and girls dance, holding each other real close grinding their hips together to the slow jams (music). I was not a very good grinder, but I tried to improve. As a teen boy with no parental guidance, the streets mostly influenced how I learned to socialize with girls. Everything I knew about girls, I learned from other boys who bragged about how they got laid.

I was quickly becoming obsessed with women. My friends and I would hang out at the subway station trying to flirt with good-looking women. Man was I barking up the wrong tree with this behavior. I already had my daddy's womanizer gene and I was putting it into full swing.

This chapter represents the avocado I would put on my wish sandwich. It offers rich, creamy flavor with the health benefits of added nutrients and antioxidants.

CHAPTER 4

Goodbye Woodycrest

Around the spring of 1964, my daddy decided he would bring Butch and I home, back to Brooklyn. Bubby had moved out on his own. I was 15 going on 16 when I left Woodycrest. I started high school at Eli Whitney in Brooklyn. I met my first girlfriend, Sara there. She was tall with brown skin, and very pretty. I used to walk her home after school when we got off the train. She lived near Utica Avenue, which was miles from where I lived. But I liked her and walking her home didn't seem so far, especially when I would get a goodbye kiss. There was a time as I was walking toward the train station at Utica Avenue, I saw my mama's boyfriend. Apparently, he lived adjacent to the station. He recognized me and cursed at me, and told me I better not come there anymore. Although I was afraid of him, I liked my girlfriend too much to not walk her home. I saw my mama there one time, and she didn't even acknowledge me. It was almost like we were strangers. I didn't see her again until two years later.

My daddy complained a lot about having to feed us. My brothers Butch, Pete, and I lived at home again with daddy. He would always tell me that I was stupid and school was a waste of time. He was trying to discourage me so I would quit and go to work to help him support us. Eventually, I dropped out of the tenth grade and went to work delivering expensive fur coat buttons. I would take the train to deliver them to various drop-off locations around the city. This job didn't last long; I was only being paid one dollar and twenty-five cents per hour. My dad wasn't very happy with me after I quit. He was always mean to me anyway. He just got meaner and more abusive, and would regularly threaten to kill me.

Butch and I were getting bigger as we were maturing into young men. One night, while on another drunken binge, daddy threatened to kill us again. We were around 15 and 16 years old and not so willing to accept a beating. My dad was somewhat apprehensive about our size as well, so he would threaten to kill us with a bat or knife. Butch would stand up to him and tell daddy if he came into our room that night, he would kill him. That night I watched my brother fall asleep with his eyes open, as he was determined to watch for my dad, but he never showed up. Daddy was fearful of Butch. Butch was about 6'2" in height and about 190 lbs.

Soon after that, Butch left home to live with my older sister, who lived a few blocks away on Gates Avenue. I believe that was the first time I saw my sister in almost 11 years since mama left daddy, taking the girls with her.

I started staying away from home more and more. I had a friend named Jerome. He lived across the street, and we used to hang out and walk around the neighborhood. We would walk all the way up to Fulton Street along Washington Avenue. We would pass by my sister's house, and I would say hello to her and my brother Butch as they stood on the stoop. She knew the streets were full of trouble and would always caution me to be careful. But I was fifteen, young, dumb, and full of it.

Jerome and I would walk around Fulton Street stores window-shopping. We didn't have any money so we did more looking than buying. Brooklyn was awesome; you'd be walking along the street and soul music would be blaring from the storefronts. It would kind of put a lean and bounce in your step; checking out the gorgeous women made everything even more magical. Jerome lived with his mother and sister. I had a crush on his sister Mary. She was a beautiful black girl with long, jet-black hair and curves that wouldn't quit. I was sixteen now and in love.

Jerome's mother was very religious, and they attended church three to four times a week. So, if I wanted to see Jerome's sister, I had to see her at church. I started attending church pretty regularly with them. Over time, going to church changed my perspective on things. I still had feelings for Mary, but my purpose and focus changed more toward Jesus. Although, I had prior church experiences through Woodycrest, this interaction was different. I began to know God, to love and truly worship him.

Jerome and I hung out a lot, and just like my daddy, Jerome's dad was a drunk too. We were walking along Fulton Street when Jerome saw his dad crossing the street. He was staggering like he was drunk as he crossed. A speeding car struck his dad, knocking him several feet in the air. He came down on the hood of another car and was run over. Jerome thought his dad was dead and screamed out for help, as he ran to his father's side on the ground. The ambulance came and took his daddy to the emergency room, where he was treated for only a broken leg. He was very drunk and very lucky.

One night around 7 p.m., I was in the bathroom primping and preparing to join my friends at a party. My dad came in the bathroom, and I could smell the alcohol on his breath. He asked, "Where do you think you're going?" I said, "I'm going out with my friends." He replied angrily, "Oh, so you can't work, but yet you can go out in the streets?" "Dad, I'm going out and you can't stop me!" I said sternly. "Who you talking to boy? I'll cut your damn neck off!" he yelled as he reached into his pocket for his knife.

I saw him reaching for his knife, so I quickly pushed him aside and ran out the front door. I knew I couldn't go back there anymore. Enough was enough! I was done letting my dad hurt me, and I didn't care where I went, as long as it was far away from him. I was 15 years old.

My older brother Bubby let me live with him for a while. He was married and had two children at the time, a boy and a girl. He later had two more boys. He remarried and had two more children, another boy and girl. It was hard living with my brother and his wife. They were poor and didn't have much either. I used to hustle cigarettes for them. I made one friend in the neighborhood and we liked to hang out at the neighborhood store.

My friend's cousin, however, seemed to have an issue with me and would try to bully me. Well, I just about had it with his cousin one day and we broke out into a fistfight. After we fought, he told me I better not be there when he got back. I didn't take his threat seriously until I saw him heading back toward the store with a wrapped item in his hand. As he got closer, I saw that the wrapped item was a machete.

I ran and he chased me for miles. I was really fearful that he was going to chop me up. I ran and ran, only to look back to see him still following me. I finally lost him and made it back to Bubby's house. I told my brother what had happened. At first, he got mad at me, because he felt I was bringing trouble to his house. He told me that if the kid showed up, I was to take care of it. The kid did show up at my brother's house with a bunch of other kids calling me out. Bubby told me to come outside with him, so I did. The kid and his friends yelled threats at me, and Bubby told them all "to get the hell off" his property as he pulled out his gun. They took off running. He never fired a shot, and they never bothered me again.

My relationship with my brother was becoming strained, and he told me to look for another place. I had no job, no money, and no place to call home. I was at rock bottom; all I had was a shirt, a pair of pants, and worn-out sneakers. I was walking alone in downtown Brooklyn wondering what I was going to do. I was desperate and losing hope. As I was walking, I saw a sign that said, "Uncle Sam wants you." It was a U.S. Army recruiting center. I walked in and asked the recruiter, "What do I gotta do to get out of here?"

The recruiter told me that I had to pass a written test, and since I was only sixteen, I had to get a parent signature to sign me in when I turned seventeen.

Mixed Feelings

It was in the fall before my seventeenth birthday when I reunited with my mother again after 11 years of being separated. She was living in the Bedford Stevenson neighborhood in Brooklyn. She had left her previous boyfriend and was now living with another man, along with my seven brothers and sisters.

I wasn't about to go back to my abusive father to ask for his signature to enlist me into the U.S. Army, so my next best option was to approach my estranged mother. I was happy to see my mother. She tried very hard to be motherly toward me. It felt a little awkward. I knew she was my mother, but my relationship with her was distant. I think she loved me, but it is difficult for me to understand how she could love me and leave me at the same time. All I could think of is why, why did you leave me? Did I remind her of daddy, the man she hated, the same way we reminded daddy of mama when he beat the crap out of us? This was an emotionally painful reacquaintance, and just as emotional even now as I think about it.

I needed my mother for one reason, and one reason only— to sign my induction papers into the military. She tried to discourage me by saying, "Buster, there's a war going on, and you might get hurt." I told her, "There is a war going on here in Brooklyn, Mama. At least in the military they're gonna give me a gun and room and board." She went on to ask why I didn't get my dad to sign me in. I told her that daddy kicked me out, and I no longer knew where he was, nor did I care. She reluctantly signed the papers, and let me stay there periodically until I turned seventeen.

This chapter represents the pepper seasoning I put on my wish sandwich that adds spicy flavor while making me sweat a bit.

CHAPTER 4

Uncle Sam Wants You

In January 1966, I turned seventeen years old, and two weeks later I entered the United States Military. I was sworn into the U.S Army at Fort Dix in New Jersey. I was so proud to be in a position to serve my country. Not everybody that applies to serve gets approved. I felt accomplished somehow by being selected, and for passing all of the exams. Maybe this was going to open up new possibilities for me.

The induction process was quite overwhelming, however. They lined us new recruits up at the process center to get our physical examinations, heads shaved, and showers. We were issued army clothing and boots. We were instructed to line up around the room for immunizations. They applied the shots with a gun to the upper arm. Some recruits dropped to the floor unconscious after receiving the shots. I was hoping I wouldn't pass out, and fortunately I didn't have a reaction. After the induction process was over, I was officially told that I was now property of the U.S. Military.

Fort Dix was a huge army post, and I was hoping that I would be assigned there for basic training. When the recruiter gave me my test results, he said I qualified for several military occupations. Being excited and naïve, I asked him what he would suggest, because I had no idea. He said infantry would give me faster promotion (rank and salary). He said I would be a weapons expert in small arms and a fighting soldier.

When I was a kid, I used to watch a lot of war movies. One movie in particular, that had a big influence on me was the movie, *To Hell and Back*, starring Audie Murphy as a war hero.

They always made the soldiers seem macho and glamorous. So, because I always wanted to be a fighting soldier, I signed up for the infantry. I also told the recruiter that I wanted to be assigned overseas in Germany. They had other plans, however, and they assigned me to Fort Carson, Colorado, for basic training.

My plane arrived at Colorado Springs Airport. We were bussed to Fort Carson, which was about a 30-minute drive from the airport. Colorado was totally different from Brooklyn. I was accustomed to seeing skyscrapers and concrete every-where. Now, I was looking at giant mountains, wilderness, and open space. Culture shock and homesickness was my new reality. It didn't last long though, once the drill sergeant got ahold of us.

Every morning at 5:00 a.m., our drill sergeant would walk through the barracks yelling profanities to get us out of bed. We had to shit, shower and shave, and make our beds before reveille. In the Army, reveille is where you stand at attention while roll call is taken. We would salute the raising of the flag and then be dismissed for breakfast in the mess hall. A typi-cal breakfast consisted of eggs, bacon, cereal, and sometimes chipped beef. Most of us didn't like chipped beef, so we called it "shit on a shingle."

After breakfast we would do PT (physical training), which consisted of push-ups, jumping jacks, sit-ups, pull-ups and a 2-3-mile run. I really struggled with these physical activities. The drill sergeant was brutal. His job was to make soldiers out of us boys. His punishment for failure was more PT. We used to practically shed tears because the training was so brutal. But as the days and nights went on, I became more conditioned. I was becoming physically stronger, and men-tally smarter.

I liked going to the shooting range where I learned how to shoot an M14 rifle. I got to fire machine guns and throw hand grenades. We had to enter into a tear gas chamber and remove our gas mask to experience what tear gas felt like. It burned my skin and eyes, and it was difficult to breathe.

We attended instructional classes where we learned about military rules and responsibilities, and how to setup fire zones that allowed us to kill for maximum effectiveness. We learned how to read maps, plot grid coordinates, and read a compass. We did a lot of walking. We'd go in the field for weeks practicing combat maneuvers and war games.

Some field exercises were fun and exhilarating, like escape and evasion. That is a simulated war game where you were part of a small team trying to avoid capture by the enemy. Usually, this took place in the dark of night in the middle of open range. Everything was made to seem realistic. You had to crawl under barbed wire while simulated explosions would go off around you, and they would be shooting blanks to make it seem even more realistic.

Fort Carson was frigid during the winter. We were in a war game simulation one night, and it was so cold the vehicles had frost all over them. I was freezing, and they wouldn't let us start a fire or start our vehicles so we could get warm. I was miserably cold, and I was thinking that if this was real, I would probably surrender. I don't remember how it ended, but I was so glad when it did. This was one of those extreme Army endurance tests they put you through to enhance your breaking point.

Being in the Army was similar to being at Woodycrest, with all the regiments and disciplines. The years of living with my abusive father also helped condition me for survival. I had become quite independent as a young man, and I struggled with being told what to do. If I didn't agree with a commander's course of action, I would question it. This type of attitude doesn't align well with military values or chain of command. Orders are not to be questioned. I was young, defiant, and becoming more arrogant as my confidence grew.

I completed the basic training and graduated onto Advanced Infantry Training (AIT) at Fort Carson. AIT focused more specifically on weaponry. This entailed learning how to fire mortars (bombs launched from a freestanding tube), to hit enemy targets at great distances. Mortars had a vast killing radius from just a single round. I was also taught how to fire a 90-millimeter Bazooka. It was a shoulder-held weapon that delivered a large payload so powerful it could knock down a building or disable a vehicle.

Learning how to be a combat soldier at this level was both exhilarating and fascinating. My unit was the 5th Mechanized Armored Personnel Division. Part of the AIT included learning how to operate and command armored vehicles. I liked the idea of being transported by armored vehicles for two reasons. We didn't have to walk everywhere when patrolling for the enemy, and it provided cover from gunfire.

The recruiter was correct when he said I would move up the ranks fast in infantry. I went from Private E-1, the lowest grade, to Sergeant E-5 in 18 months. I was definitely a fast learner and was good at following orders when I wanted to. I didn't like being reprimanded in front of everybody, or being made a spectacle of. My defiant nature and arrogance was still a challenge.

When I made the rank of Specialist E-4, I became squad leader, right under the rank of platoon sergeant. A platoon had 32 men. There were four squads of eight men making up the platoon. There were four platoons that made up a Company Command, four Companies to a Battalion, and two Battalions to a Division. As a squad leader, I commanded an Armored Personnel Carrier (APC). The APC was like a miniature tank on tracks. The APC could hold one squad and all the gear and weapons that a squad would be armed with. As the squad leader, I was responsible to learn everything about the vehicle including driving it, manning the machine gun turret, and maintaining radio contact with other units.

Once when we were out on a practice war maneuver, I was manning the machine gun turret while the driver suddenly stopped the vehicle, launching me headfirst out of the turret and over the front of the APC. I landed on my head. I didn't get hurt, but boy was my ego bruised. I yelled and reprimanded the driver. He then explained that the differential on the APC broke, locking up the brakes, and it wasn't his fault. There are always accidents in the military; some are deadly. We had to know and respect that these munitions could accidently explode, and equipment could fail, leading to injury. But I was young, still seventeen and invulnerable, or so I thought.

Making A Friend

I graduated from AIT and was placed in a permanent unit at Fort Carson. I still trained and had physical fitness every day. I lived in a barrack and basically worked every day like a regular job. At 5 p.m. I was off-duty and free to do whatever I wanted, as long as I didn't have guard duty. I spent a lot of my off-duty time at the post social club. I taught myself how to play the saxophone and was getting pretty good.

I met a civilian who worked at the social club named Bayman. We became friends and we talked a lot. I guess he was intrigued that I was a teenage soldier from New York. He was only nineteen himself. We developed this teenage bond. I was quite lonesome most of the time, because most of the soldiers were older than me and had different social interests. So, I just hung out with my new friend Bayman.

One weekend, he invited me to his home to meet his family in Colorado Springs. I was delighted to meet his family and they were all very nice to me. Over time, they adopted me as part of their family and I adopted them as well. Bayman had a foxy sister named Jean, who I liked a lot. Nobody in the world looked as good as her in bellbottom pants. She was hot. She was 15 years old and I was 17 years old when we were introduced.

Her family, with a few exceptions, loved God and went to church regularly. I had some past experience with God, so I started going to church again during my time off from duty. Jean and I started dating. I would walk from Fort Carson to see her which was about 15 miles or so. Bayman's siblings used to play softball in their backyard and Jean would love it. I was getting real comfortable with my new family. On some weekends I would go to parties with Jean and we would dance and have lots of fun. I wasn't Jean's only admirer though. There were at least three other boys trying to vie for her affection. I had a slight advantage, because I stayed overnight at the family home quite often. Jean and I became very close, and we would make out for hours. I was still a virgin, and all that making out got me pretty excited.

Bayman was a good friend in his own way. You could say we were odd best friends. He liked to get into fights with people. When I was with him during those violent times, I would have to remind him I was in the army and they could kick me out for unbecoming behavior. But, I still liked hanging out with him because we were close in age, and we were drinking buddies.

He showed me a lot of things in life that seemed like fun, but as I realized later, weren't decent or moral. I remember a time when we were together with one of his other friends, and we picked up this neighborhood girl who liked him. He was quite the lady's man and he knew it. He would refer to women as skunks and bitches. I never corrected him, I just silently disagreed. We rode around with this girl while drinking and partying in the car. Bayman encouraged the girl to offer herself sexually to all of us. She agreed to have sex with everybody but me, so I just watched as the others mounted her in the back seat. I had strong feelings for Jean anyway, so I was okay with not being involved.

I told my platoon sergeant about Jean and asked him if I could borrow his car to go see her. He said okay. He was really cool to do that. He didn't even ask me if I knew how to drive or if I had a driver's license. Good thing he didn't because I had no license and never drove a car on the streets before. I dented his car by accidently turning too sharp and hitting a guard rail as I was driving out of the parking lot.

I made it safely to Jean's house and then drove her up to lover's point. She was dying laughing because she knew I didn't know how to drive very well and didn't have a license. She thought I was crazy and daring. I made it back to the post and paid for the damages to Sarg's car.

I was getting close to being 18 years old when I got called into my commander's office. He instructed me to begin preparing for my deployment to Vietnam. I was feeling uneasy about this, because I knew there was a war going on, and I could get hurt or killed over there. But reality set in, and I had to accept my deployment because it was my duty. I was given a 30-day leave, which I spent with Jean. I said goodbye to my Colorado family and friends.

I was flown to Fort Lewis, Washington, to join up with the 4th Infantry Division. The entire unit was being transported to Vietnam via Navy ship. In preparing for my departure with the unit, I was issued all essential combat gear. We were about to board the ship when I got orders to stand down, because the President of the United States issued a decree prohibiting soldiers serving in combat zones under 18 years old. I was 17½ years old and was reassigned to a unit at Fort Lewis. It was a blessing, because as I learned later, my previous unit, the 4th Infantry Division took on a lot of casualties in Vietnam. Most everyone in the unit had no real combat experience. Everything was learned through trial and error. They lost a lot of young soldiers.

I remained at Fort Lewis for about six months. I remember waking up every morning seeing this huge mountain staring me right in the face. This mountain was Mt. Rainier and it was spectacular. I went to the neighboring cities, Seattle and Tacoma, a few times with some GI buddies.

South Korea

I received new deployment orders, but not to Vietnam. I was being sent to South Korea. In 1967, I was assigned to the 7th Infantry Division in Dongducheon, Camp Casey. The barracks where we lived was a Quonset (dome) type building. There were multiple Quonset buildings used for living quarters, storage, bathrooms and Company Command office. A pedestrian bridge expanding the creek bed provided access to the sleeping quarters from the command office and mess hall. We had a Korean houseboy who shined our boots, did our laundry, and cleaned our barracks. My houseboy's name was Kim. He was a kind, friendly, and hard-working man.

Soon after being assigned to Camp Casey, I applied to attend the non-commissioned officer academy located in Seoul, in hopes of a receiving a promotion. This was an advanced infantry skills combat training and leadership program. I was accepted and completed the program within 90 days. I was then promoted to Sergeant E-5. I was proud and excited of all my accomplishments at 18 years old.

When I returned to my unit at Camp Casey, I was assigned to be platoon sergeant. I was now the leader of 32 men, and responsible for their lives. I felt up to the task, but I was young and still had a lot of growing up to do. I became close with two of my squad leaders. They introduced me to smoking marijuana. Smoking it made me laugh. Everything was so funny. It also made me feel so good and relaxed. We thought we were inconspicuous when we would hide in places to smoke it, but I suspected others knew we were getting high. It seemed like a lot of soldiers were getting high, or drunk, or both. Military command was trying to crack down on drug and alcohol use, especially illegal drugs.

My men enjoyed my leadership style because I was more relaxed and fun than most platoon sergeants. One day, while performing marching drills with my platoon, I was getting a little jazzy with my cadence. "Left, left, left, right, left." "When I get my three-day pass," I shouted. My men would retort by repeating each phrase. "I'm gonna kick ol' Jody's ass!" "If Jody is seven feet tall," "I ain't gonna mess with him at all!" "Am I right or wrong?" My men chanted, "You're right!" as they stepped on their right leg. I then went on to shout, "Sound off!" They retorted, "One, two, three, four, one two, THREE, FOUR!"

My new Company Commander, who was really uptight, didn't seem to appreciate my leadership style. He heard our cadence and came out of his office. He stomped over to me and yelled in my face, "Knock this shit off, Bowden! This ain't your ghetto neighborhood! This is the U.S. Army! You're not leading a bunch of monkeys, you're leading a bunch of soldiers! Now, dismiss your men!" I was angry and humiliated by the way he reprimanded me in front of my men.

Korea was cold during the winter. It was so cold when we would go on long simulated combat patrols, we wore special insulated rubber boots to keep our feet warm and prevent frostbite. We called them Mickey Mouse boots. They were heavy and required extra effort walking in them. In the 1960s this rural area of South Korea was undeveloped. Korean people lived in hooches made of wood with aluminum tin roofs constructed from empty soda cans. They had open gray water drain systems meandering throughout their villages. They used outhouses for solid waste deposits.

The town center is where merchants conducted business, particularly to earn the American soldier's dollars. You could buy a tailor-made suit for four Korean won, equivalent to twenty dollars. A lot of soldiers would buy wares and ship them home for when they returned. It wasn't the best quality, but it was cheap. There were photography studios, restaurants, and lots of jewelry stores. You could buy anything, and if they didn't have what you were looking for, they would send a runner to go get it and bring it back for you.

Another popular pastime for us soldiers was to hang out at the local night clubs. The clubs played American music, and the Korean women would dress up like models to make you forget all about home. Many of these Korean women wanted to seduce you into marrying them, so that you would take them home with you when you left South Korea.

I met a Korean girl named Scoshe Kim. She was petite and had a great smile. We decided to date. I paid for her room and board in the village so when I visited, we would have a place to eat and sleep together. She was called my "yeobo" in Korean. Lots of soldiers had yeobos. These types of relationships had their advantages over sleeping around with various sexual partners, which some GIs preferred. Venereal diseases were pretty rampant.

Being 18 years old, sex for me was like being a kid in a candy store. I was addicted, and couldn't get enough. Kim taught me how to speak Korean, and I picked it up pretty fast. I was so good at speaking and understanding the language, that I could actually sing Korean songs very well. The locals loved my smooth, silky voice, and invited me to sing at the Walker Hill Resort in Seoul. I would emulate popular Korean pop artists and the locals would cheer loudly, and give me standing ovations.

I also astounded many of my Korean soldier friends with my singing talent. They would invite me to sing at their socials. We would sit around the table and drink "makgeolli" (rice wine), while singing drinking songs in Korean.

Drinking and drug use was something I did more often. Scoshe Kim and I ended up breaking up which made me sad, so I got drunk and popped some pills called red-devils. Next thing I knew, I was waking up in the post infirmary (medical hospital). I didn't get reprimanded because this happened on my personal time; however, I stayed away from the village after that and never saw Scoshe Kim again. Little did I know that I was heading down a self-destructive path.

It was my second year in South Korea. We were preparing for a big war simulation training. We packed up all our gear into rucksacks (large military style back packs), weighing upwards of 60 pounds when fully packed. We were a mechanized division, so we packed everything into the APC vehicles and headed into battle. Our objective was to capture the enemy-occupied mountain.

My company commander wasn't good at strategic combat planning. Instead of taking us to the base of the mountain in the APC to embark and attack, he decided to embark a mile away, and run us on foot to the base of the mountain. We ran with rucksacks on our backs, rifle in hand, through a wet creek bed and open terrain. Then we had to climb the mountain to engage the enemy. We were half dead just from the run alone by the time we reached the base of the mountain. This tactic exposed us out in the open to enemy fire.

I was tagged out as being killed in the simulation. My role was over, I was out of action. I was kind of glad that I was tagged because this commander was going to literally kill me just by the physical demand of his tactics. The company commander seemed to have had it in for me for some time. We were in the field on another occasion, and the company commander called me out in front of my men. I didn't like it and he knew it. So, he gave me an order to do something, and I refused. I was pissed off and defiant. He charged me with disobeying a direct order, and I found myself court-martialed. A court-martial is a military-held trial and prosecution. I was found guilty and sentenced to six months in the stockade (jail), and forfeiture of rank and pay. I was devastated and angry. I was nineteen years old, in jail, in a foreign country.

My attitude worsened and I would get into fights with other inmates and the military guards. I was totally rebelling and out of control. The military has ways to break you. They put me in solitary confinement. This was a four-foot by six-foot metal box with a cot for sleeping. The lighting was low and the only source of light was during the day, when the sunlight would shine through a tiny little window high up in the cell. There was no one to talk to. I was so depressed and alone. I felt caged like an animal, and it fueled my anger. How could they treat me like that? I was only nineteen and had never been in jail before. I yelled at the top of my lungs, hurting in mental anguish. I was in and out of solitary confinement, because I became more defiant and vindictive.

When my jail sentence ended, I soon returned to the United States and was reassigned to Fort Carson, Colorado, again. I reconnected with Bayman and Jean. I kept in touch with Jean while in Korea. We started dating again and things were going well. I was young and impressionable. Bayman got married, so I thought I would too. Jean and I got married in 1970, and I thought if things didn't work out, I could always get a divorce.

This chapter represents the lettuce of my wish sandwich, providing crunch and much-needed fiber.

CHAPTER 5

Vietnam

We were married for only six months when I got my orders to go to Vietnam. It happened so fast! I said my goodbyes again and boarded the plane to Oakland Army Depot in California for overseas processing. While there, I saw guys returning from Vietnam. Some were still in their dusty combat fatigues transported directly from the jungle to the States. They were very happy, as you can imagine, to be back in the U.S. They survived being in a war. They shared stories with me of what to expect. The best advice I kept getting was to keep my head down. I was feeling apprehensive, but knew I had no choice but to go. To be honest, I was curious and wanted to see what war was like.

I had about a week of free time while waiting for my flight to Vietnam, so I decided to explore San Francisco. What a magnificent city. I went to the Fillmore District, the music mecca for black folks. I fell in love with San Francisco and the beautiful women I encountered. I was in uniform and telling people I was heading to Vietnam. The people embraced me, bought me drinks, and helped make my time there even more enjoyable. It was surreal, almost like I was living a movie. I thought to myself, "If I make it back from Vietnam, I think I would like to live in San Francisco."

It was August 1970, and the plane was packed with replacement soldiers, myself included, headed for Vietnam. It was a long flight. Our first stop was Anchorage, Alaska. I got off the plane at the Anchorage Airport to stretch my legs. The gift shop in the terminal had this gigantic stuffed polar bear. I was quite fascinated with it. Pondering, "Here's the kid from Brooklyn, now in Alaska." Our next stop was Tokyo, Japan. I was surprised at how small the Japanese appeared next to the giant planes and refueling trucks. Japanese people are typically small in comparison to Americans, but I had never experienced it firsthand.

The flight was long over the Pacific and looking through the window, I saw lots of islands below us throughout the flight. We were fed roast beef sandwiches, which reminded me of water buffalo meat, because that is what we heard was a staple in Asia. Finally, we approached Vietnam and were preparing to land at Saigon Airport. I couldn't help but notice the many bomb craters in the earth as we descended. I was able to make out the huts in which the Vietnamese lived. As we got closer to the ground, I saw people in black pajamas and straw hats. This was customary attire for the Vietnamese. I could see smoke billowing from fires on the ground, which made this dreaded landing in a war zone seem even more eerie and surreal. As we got off the plane, I was feeling a little uneasy. I probably wasn't the only one.

We were given a welcome speech and were told to follow orders. We loaded up on buses to Bien Hoa Army processing center. The post was an hour ride from the airport. It was very strange, because we were in a war zone where people were being killed, riding in a tour bus. I began to wonder how many of us riding on that bus wouldn't make it back home alive. I began thinking how easy it would be for the enemy to blow up the bus or shoot us through the windows of the bus. My danger instincts were kicking in, and I began looking very closely at the people in the villages as we passed by. I thought, "I've entered a real war zone, no letting my guard down from here on." We arrived at Bien Hoa. We were issued jungle combat fatigues, given orientation and told the do's and don'ts.

We were told to practice abstinence because sexually transmitted diseases were widespread. We were given malaria pills and told to be sure to take them daily, because you can easily die from the mosquito-carrying disease. We were also warned that the enemy uses children and woman to get you to lower your guard. They have been known to throw hand grenades and provide distractions for attacks. We were shown examples of weapons and booby traps that the enemy used to kill us. It was really beginning to get worrisome as we acclimated to our new reality.

These booby traps consisted of unexploded U.S. bombs, and punji sticks (sharpened bamboo-like spears), placed in obscure locations designed to impale you as you patrolled through the jungle. Fortified bunkers were located on the perimeter of the post, where we rotated men on guard. We were given fully loaded M-16 automatic assault rifles. It didn't take long to start bonding and making friends with other soldiers. Bien Hoa was a processing center, which assigned replacement soldiers to bases located all over the country.

Part of the orientation was learning the geography. We were currently in the southern part of Vietnam. The enemy in this area were referred to as guerrillas (Vietcong). They were North Vietnamese sympathizers acting as soldiers against the United States. They were not typically in uniform. They lived amongst the general population in support of the Communist effort or were just anti-American. You couldn't tell them apart from the other black pajama-wearing Vietnamese, unless they had a gun in their hand. They were organized and operated just like trained professional soldiers. The northern half of Vietnam was under the control and occupied by the Communist enemy. Hanoi, North Vietnam, was the capital and headquarters of this opposing Communist army.

The area which separated the North from the South was where we fought uniformed, Vietnamese soldiers that were trained to kill, just like us. They were strategic, and they fought hard. Word had gotten around at Bien Hoa that up north isn't where you want to be assigned, because the mortality rate was much higher there. It was also known that the fighting was intense. Unless you had a death wish, this was an area to avoid.

I received orders placing me in the 101st Airborne Division at a base named Camp Eagle at Phu Bai, Northern Vietnam. Everyone was looking at the map on the wall to see where they were being assigned. One of the guys asked me where I was heading, and I told him Phu Bai. He looked on the map and said, "You can kiss your ass goodbye!" I tried to get reassigned because I thought they made a mistake, because I wasn't Airborne Infantry, I was Mechanized Infantry. I was told that meant I was mobile, and to pack my gear.

There were three of us assigned to Phu Bai, and we proceeded to board a C130 military aircraft transport. We landed in Da Nang, South Vietnam, and boarded a Huey helicopter bound for Camp Eagle, Phu Bai. The terrain was hilly and heavy with vegetation, more so than in the south. Vietnam is a beautiful country. It is very tropical, buggy, and humid. The country has many varieties of wildlife. They have Indian elephants, black bears and honey bears, Indochinese tigers and leopards, and smaller animals like monkeys, bats, flying squirrels, turtles and otters. Because some of the terrain was swampland, it also had reptiles such as crocodiles and snakes. The deadliest of snakes was the bamboo viper. We nicknamed it the one stepper. If it bit you, one step later you were dead.

I was assigned to Firebase Bastogne near the A Shau Valley, a major supply route that was controlled by enemy combatants. There were many big battles in this area. Firebase Bastogne was a forward combat operations command. Base camp was where the Company, Battalion, and Division Headquarters are located, typically referred to as the "rear." The rear provided logistics and tactical support, field hospital, clothing and food supplies, armory, helicopter transports, and helicopter gunships. Before I was sent to the field or Firebase, the Army required me to go through P-training. This training was specific to what you may encounter in the jungle or in the field. In the field you would encounter villages or rice patties, so they would tell us what to watch for when encountering various scenarios like the following: how to be cautious and vigilant when making contact with locals; how to identify booby traps and ambushes in the jungle; and also to be aware of every step.

The simulated P-training entailed walking through a makeshift jungle. The trainers had placed booby traps and disguised tunnels and choggy holes (places where the enemy snipers would hide to shoot you from). The trainer told me it was my turn to walk point. Point is the position of being in front making first contact, and calling out traps and detecting tunnels, etc. The trainer made a comment that I better be sharp because I made "a pretty big target." I didn't like his comment and didn't think it was appropriate. I proceeded to walk through the makeshift jungle, and the trainer pointed out the things I didn't detect that would have injured or killed me in a real situation. I didn't feel very confident after that.

The infantry were responsible for ground security around the bases. I remember my first guard post and how eerie it was. It started as soon as the sun went down and lasted all night. There was an entire company of soldiers in fox holes with rifles, machine guns and grenade launchers all pointing downrange toward the enemy. There were rows of barbed wire around the perimeter in front of our positions. The Vietnamese used their soldiers as human bombs; we called them "sappers." They would be strapped with explosives and try to infiltrate our perimeter, and blow themselves up along with anyone in the vicinity.

On my first night of combat assignment, I was assigned with two other soldiers to man a forward outpost. The outpost was two to three hundred yards in front of the perimeter where all weapons were pointed. The idea of being in front of all that firepower didn't sit well with us, considering how nervous and trigger-happy everyone was. We wanted to discuss the sense of walking out in front of all that firepower, but the officer in charge didn't want to hear our point of view. He gave us a direct order to man the outpost.

Just as we were heading to the outpost, gunfire erupted from the foxholes. I took position in the trench and commenced firing my grenade launcher. A cease-fire was ordered, and we stopped firing. They illuminated the area and no evidence of intrusion was found. Turns out that someone thought they saw something and started shooting, and then everyone else started shooting too. If we had gone out to the outpost as commanded, we would have been downrange from all that firepower, and likely wouldn't be here today. The perimeter commander called off the forward observation assignment for that night. I was relieved to not have to go out there after that.

As I became more acclimated to my surroundings, I adjusted to the reality of war, and the fact that I may get killed. But, I just buried those feelings. After a while, I just stopped caring, because going home was such a long way off. My heart began to harden as I was faced with the realities of war, kill or be killed. We had a one-year deployment obligation before we could rotate home. Soldiers died and were injured routinely, and we would get reports through the grapevine of guys we knew getting killed or injured. I think every soldier had their own way of dealing with loss and stress; most turned to alcohol or drugs to cope with the intensity of war.

I started using scag (heroin). Everybody else was doing it because it took the edge off. I felt so mentally and emotionally screwed up. There were times when the sirens sounded, notifying us of incoming rocket attack and to take cover. I was so high that I wouldn't take cover. In fact, I found these attacks rather annoying because they would interfere with my high.

I reluctantly boarded the Huey helicopter that flew me to the front, Firebase Bastogne, which was the combat field operations support. The base was located on top of a hill, heavily fortified with a battalion of infantry soldiers with some of the biggest artillery guns I had ever seen. These huge guns were placed strategically along the hilltop. They had enormous explosive power and range, and were really loud like a bomb going off. They were used in support of U.S. Infantry operations in the field.

When I first arrived, I was taken on a tour of the area in an open jeep. As I looked around, I couldn't help but notice the thick vegetation: thick brushy areas where the enemy could hide and take shots at you. I was feeling apprehensive about being so openly exposed, but the lieutenant taking us on tour seemed to be very comfortable and unintimidated. He pointed out several major battle landmarks where lots of soldiers lost their lives. He pointed to hill 882 where a major battle took place to capture this territory. Then he pointed toward the A Shau Valley, a major access point for the North Vietnamese soldiers. He finished his orientation with, "Many people were killed here during the 1968 'Tet' offensive."

I was thoroughly fearful after that tour and convinced I had entered into hell. We rode back to the Firebase and I was introduced to the men in my platoon, and told I would be going on patrol the next day. We slept in bunkers and took turns for a two-hour watch. Some nights were like daylight and other nights it was so dark you couldn't see your hand in front of your face. Vietnam's climate was hot all the time even during the monsoon season when it rained constantly. The next morning, in preparation for patrol, we were assigned weapons. Some guys carried M16 automatic rifles, some carried grenade launchers, someone would carry the M60 Machine Gun, and someone carried the 90mm recoilless rifle (like a Bazooka). The M60 and Bazooka were the heaviest and most powerful weapons in the squad. Because of my size, I was given those weapons to carry on patrol.

We headed down the road away from the firebase, walking single file, prepared for a fight. Being the new guy, I had the jitters and was on total alert. We had walked for some distance when we came upon a village. The people in the village were dressed simply. The men and woman wore tunics, cloth that covered their genital area, and were bare-chested. They were friendly and seemed to not care or understand what the fighting was all about. Those people were Montagnards, an indigenous community in Vietnam. We returned to the Firebase without making enemy contact.

One night while on ambush patrol, there was a loud explosion that alerted everyone. An ambush was where we set traps at night to kill the enemy. They were known to be more active at night, because they could move about much easier undetected. The patrol leader radioed to the Firebase for an illumination round to be fired over our position on the ground, so we could see what triggered the booby trap. We were very intense and alert, always expecting the worse. We moved very cautiously toward what looked like a body from a distance; however, once we were able to clearly see, it was just an animal. The animal I learned was called a banana cat. It resembled a raccoon and a cat. I'm pretty certain the enemy knew we set up ambushes along roads and commonly traveled paths. They probably avoided these areas and traveled through tunnels that were obscure and undetectable.

I was in Vietnam for about three months before my first encounter with death. I was on base when these soldiers, U.S allied patrol, walked by me carrying three dead bodies tied to wooden poles, similar to how people carry a deer kill out of the woods. The sight was shockingly disturbing.

As time passed, I became more and more crazy. One day while on the Firebase, I heard over the radio that some of our guys were caught in friendly fire. When the helicopter arrived with the wounded, I saw my buddy, Sgt. LaBoy being transported off, and he was not wounded. He was dead. I was mortified! He was my friend. I couldn't believe that he was killed, especially at the hands of our own troops! The white soldiers that were being transported back were so badly burned by the exploding rounds, that I couldn't tell if they were white or black. I was so enraged that this could happen! I felt like I was losing my mind!

That night on the Firebase, just like everyone that wasn't on duty, I started drinking and got drunk. Some white artillery soldiers said some insensitive, derogatory slurs to me and my black friends, and fists started flying. One of my infantry buddies pulled a knife out and the artillery officer pointed his rifle at us, threatening to shoot. I was standing close to the rifle being pointed at us, so I hit it up into the air and punched the guy. The gun fell to the ground, and I encouraged my buddies to leave with me. I headed out to grab a grenade. I was planning to toss it at them, when thank God the sergeant major talked me down from being so angry. He asked what happened. I explained they insulted us, calling us "niggers," and that started the fight. He said he was placing me under house arrest and that I could return to my unit in the morning.

The Black College of Knowledge

In the morning I was told that charges were being brought against me and my black friend who brandished the knife. We were the only ones charged. We weren't charged for the fight on the hill with the artillery soldiers though. We were charged with disobeying an order from an officer. I said to them, "I never disobeyed an order that I heard given to me." Nevertheless, this was a serious charge in a war zone, and we were both court-martialed and sentenced to six months in a military jail in Saigon, Vietnam. We were air transported from Phu Bai to the Da Nang stockade. I felt betrayed and a victim of racial injustice.

There were a lot of bitter, young black soldiers in the Da Nang stockade. At least 90% were black marines and U.S Army soldiers. Most, I believe were confined for insubordination or some other offense against the military code of justice. Some were even there for murder. Some of the prisoners, particularly the Marine population, were so violently hateful and angry, that they kept them locked up in maximum security confinement. I used to hear them at night chanting, "White man snow, stay the f*** away from my door." This would go on for hours. Then you could hear brawls and alarms going off that signaled to other guards that a riot was in progress and help was needed.

I hated the American military now, more than I hated the enemy. I wasn't alone in feeling this way. Being locked in jail is hard enough, but being locked up in a war zone at the hands of your own countrymen was hopelessly hard. The Vietnamese were smart; they knew we were racially divided within our ranks and country. They played that up to pit us against each other. They would disseminate propaganda pamphlets high-lighting racial injustice, and say things like, "They don't want to kill us, the black soldier," and, "Your fight is at home."

For 30 days, I was locked up in a little 4 feet by 6 feet cell. My cell was next to another black soldier. I can't remember his name, but he could sing like Otis Redding. When he sang, we would reminisce, thinking of home. He was from San Antonio, Texas. He even believed he was a reincarnation of Otis Redding. We started singing together, and the other inmates would love it.

I learned that I was being transferred to LBJ, Long Binh Jail in Saigon. LBJ, aka "The Black College of Knowledge," was the name black soldiers gave to the prison. When I arrived at LBJ, the first thing I noticed was how big it was. The fence was constructed of twenty-foot sections of corrugated metal, wrapped with dark green canvas, so you couldn't see in or out. There were gun towers towering above the height of the fence located every fifty to one hundred feet. I would guess that it encompassed five square city blocks. Once inside the facility, we were segregated by high security and medium security. Like most black American prisoners, I was considered high-risk because of my militant attitude. I was angry, rebellious, and insubordinate. Even in jail, conflict was a part of my world. I was trained to kill, and I had disregard for human life. In light of my circumstances, taking orders or being told what to do was my Achilles heel.

When I was not intimated by the authorities, I did well. There was a yard area where we made concrete bricks. There was a dormitory-like cell block environment where we were housed. During the day we would be assigned clean-up work or some other manual labor. After work hours we were allowed to mingle in the yard. Some of us would use this time to write letters home. At times, we would even go outside the prison accompanied with armed guards to do cleanup along the roadside. The Vietnamese would look at us knowing we were prisoners. Even though at times we would hear gunfire and explosions, we never felt threatened. The enemy knew we were out of commission, and jailed soldiers benefited their psychological warfare goal, to divide and conquer.

The Army used black prison guards to try to keep us suppressed. I remember being assaulted by a black prison guard in solitary confinement. Solitary confinement was cruel punishment. They put me in a 6 feet by 6 feet metal shipping container. The container was modified with one opening with bars. There was no bathroom or water within the container. The guards would let you out to shower and use the toilet. You'd shower and use the toilet in open view of the guard. Despite my pessimistic outlook, the photos and letters I received from home gave me something positive to look forward to. I stayed six months in Long Binh Jail. It was an experience like nothing you could imagine.

The unfair treatment I received in the U.S Army just alienated me further. To expect me to give up my life for a country that treated me as an unequal, third-class citizen did not inspire me to want to die for it. The worst of all was being locked up and treated like an animal while in a war zone. I made some mistakes, and I can own up to that. I should have received treatment, not jail time.

Prior to being released from jail, a colonel reviewed my case and interviewed me before making his recommendation. He recognized that I had made some significant accomplishments during my five years in the military. He asked me what I wanted to do. There were two options: I could return to a combat unit and finish out my tour of duty, or I could be dishonorably discharged from the military and sent home. Tearfully, I said that I couldn't serve anymore after being unjustly treated, locked up, and abused. I stated, "I came into the military proud and honored to serve my country, but now I'm just broken. Please send me home. I don't care about the type of discharge."

I can remember looking at the colonel as he said to me, "You've been through enough. I am going to recommend a "General Discharge under Honorable Conditions." This colonel had a great heart and helped me out greatly by giving me another chance at life. I attribute my success and who I am today to his merciful heart. Colonel, if you are reading this story and remember the kid to whom you gave a second chance, thank you, thank you from the bottom of my heart. You represent the America we should all fight and be willing to die for. God Bless you, Sir!

This chapter represents the pickles that give my wish sandwich extra crunch and zing.

CHAPTER 6

Civilian Life

The flight home was long. We hit some bad weather, thunder and lightning that lit up the night sky. The plane shook, rocked and dropped. Did I survive Vietnam only to die in a plane crash? The plane eventually landed at McCord Air Force Base in Washington. It was culture shock all over again. I was used to being in a primitive environment, and here I was seeing modern cars that made me feel like I just walked into the future.

I was flown to Fort Dix, New Jersey, where I received my discharge papers from the military, since that is where I originally enlisted. I had been away from New York for five years. I had no desire to reconnect with any part of my past at this point of my life. I narrowly escaped the horrors of Vietnam and imprisonment, and I was not at all interested in going back to the jungles of Brooklyn. That part of my life was put away in the past. My home and my family were now in Colorado. I got on a plane and headed home to see my sweetheart and wife, Jean.

Making a life as a married man, and now as a civilian, was an adjustment. Jean and I moved out of her parent's home into an apartment. We both had jobs. I worked as a janitor and she worked as an elevator operator. We barely made enough money for rent and food. I went from job to job trying to find my occupational niche. I worked with my father-in-law's company as a concrete laborer and form setter. This work was extremely physical and exhausting. I didn't see a future in that line of work. It was fun because I worked alongside my brothers-in-law. Everything was always a competition; who was the strongest, fastest, etc. I was pretty smart and assertive, probably a carryover from my leadership role in the military. However, my father-in-law favored his own sons, and gave them more learning opportunities, and paid them more money.

Things weren't going well for me and Jean. I was always hanging out with Bayman, my brother-in-law, and getting into trouble. I would often stay out until late hours of the night, and wasn't really there for her much. Bayman was popular among the young crowd, and they looked up to him like a leader. I looked up to him too, and I wanted to be more like him. He was a gangster, and his rivals were the north side blacks, and ALL white people. He didn't trust any of them.

We had heard about some white guys pulling guns on some black guys. Bayman was the enforcer and anytime something like that went down, he would spring into action. One night there were about five of us riding in my car. I was driving, cruising down the strip, when we came alongside some white guys that started taunting us and yelling racial slurs. I sped up to avoid the confrontation; however, one of the guys in my backseat pulled out a shotgun and fired it at them. The police nearby heard the shots and hit us with their lights and sirens for us to pull over. I immediately hit the gas and tried to get away. As we were speeding down the road, one of the guys in the back threw the gun out the window.

I quickly turned into an alley, almost hitting a utility pole, only to see another cop car coming at us from that direction. I looked back, and we were trapped. The cops pinned us in and got out of their cars with their guns drawn, yelling at us to put our hands up. We all slowly got out of the car with our hands up, and they quickly grabbed us and put the cuffs on. I tried to lie my way out of it by telling the cops I just got back from Vietnam and I was having a flashback. The cop said, "What, did you think you were driving a tank?" The lie didn't help. I was convicted of a misdemeanor and sentenced to 30 days in jail for eluding a police officer.

My public defender must have had a sense that I was struggling with being misguided, struggling with adjusting to civilian life, and needed intervention. He looked me straight in the eye and told me I needed to start making better decisions, because I am a father now, and if I'm in jail I won't be able to raise my own kids.

Jean came to visit me in jail, along with our three-year-old son and infant daughter. She broke down crying, saying that my behavior was destroying our lives, our reputation, and good standing in the community. I felt terrible. I told her that I wouldn't do it again.

After getting out of jail, an acquaintance I had met through Bayman asked me if I would rob a superstore with him. I thought he was joking around, but he said, "Couldn't you use the money?" I told him, "I'll think about it and let you know." A few weeks later he asked me if I was ready. I said, "What is the plan?" He said, "You drive the getaway car and keep a lookout for the cops, and signal by blowing your horn to warn me." I have never robbed anything in my life, so all I could think about was, what if we get caught, then we would go to prison. I reluctantly said, "Okay, I'm in." The robbery would take place on a weeknight, the following week. He called me to meet him at his house. I really didn't have the nerve to do it, so I didn't show up. That night I heard on the news the superstore had been robbed and the robber got away with an undisclosed amount of money. I knew it was him. He did the robbery without me. I never heard from him again. Even though he got away with a load of cash, I was glad I wasn't a part of it.

I was determined to live a life without drama or legal trouble again. It seemed like moving my family to Denver, about 70 miles north of Colorado Springs, was a good idea. Denver was a nice place to live. It is a large metropolitan area adjacent to the east slope of the Colorado Rocky Mountains. We bought a home in a community called Park Hill, and got the kids set up in the nearby elementary school.

Having a bit of maturity under my belt, it occurred to me that it might benefit my family if they had the chance to meet some of my family in Brooklyn, New York. My father and I had spoken on the phone many times prior to our trip to New York. I felt fairly positive about our relationship now that I was a grown man with a family. We chose to stay with my dad at his apartment while we visited other family members in New York. Getting this chance to introduce my wife and kids to my New York family made me feel proud. It was good to reconnect with my family. I looked forward to building new, more positive memories with them.

Months later, while back in Denver, I received a call from my dad. We were really getting along well, so I invited him to come visit us in Denver. My family joined me to greet him at the airport since this was his first time visiting us, and it was his first time flying on an airplane. He had the biggest smile on his face when he saw us all waiting for him.

During his visit, I took him to see some of the most beautiful places around Denver. He joined us camping in Leadville, Colorado, where we went trout fishing in Turquoise Lake. My dad was blown away by the majestic views of snow-covered mountains. He seemed to have a connection with nature in this outdoor environment. He would share funny stories with me and the kids while fishing for trout. He made us all laugh, and we were becoming best of friends.

In Denver, I started working for a trucking company. I was a dirt hauler. I drove an 18-wheeler belly dump. The company was contracted to fill a valley along Highway 24, just west of a town named Woodland Park, east of Pike's Peak. I enjoyed driving the big rig and was good at it. Driving a tractor trailer filled with a load of dirt was dangerous, but I never thought about the danger until it was staring me in the face.

The way we had to approach the dump pit with the trucks loaded was at a speed that would spread the dirt evenly when the clamshell dump gates opened. After release of the dirt, we proceeded at a speed to help us climb out of the pit. The only way the trucks could climb up the steep slope after dumping was to be completely empty, because the weight of the dirt would be too heavy for the engine to pull.

On this one particular run, I released the gates as I got a thumbs up from the dump coordinator standing on the ground. I continued my momentum up the hill. I realized the truck was struggling to get up the hill. I turned my head to look back at the trailer chutes. After the dust cleared, I saw that one of the chutes was still full of dirt. Obviously, one of the gates failed to open to release the dirt. The problem, however, is once the gates are released, the air pressure drops and takes a little time to replenish. The air tank pressure also operates the brakes. No air pressure, no brakes.

Once I saw the load still in the trailer, I knew that I had to do everything I could to continue the climb. The truck was really lugging as I approached the crest of the hill. I jammed the gearshift into low-low, which is typically only accessible from a stop-to-start position. The truck died at the crest of the hill and began rolling backwards. The only thing I could do to keep it from going over the edge, or tipping over, was try to steer it so the trailer followed the path of the road. I was keeping it in line with the winding road until the speed of the truck picked up so fast that I lost control. The truck careened toward the cliff edge of the hillside, where there was soft enough dirt that it slowed the truck's momentum. The truck came to a stop just a few feet away from the edge. I was so nervous afterwards that I wanted to quit, but the operations boss gave me lots of kudos for doing a spectacular job.

I regained my composure and drove the truck down into the pit for my second attempt to dump. All went well this time, and I headed back up the hill to get another load. This was the highest paying job I had ever had, and it helped us get ahead financially. The job lasted well over a year.

During the winter months the air tanks on the trucks would freeze overnight. Temperatures in the Colorado Rockies would get down in the single digits. One winter day, we were letting our trucks warm up on a slight grade. While the trucks were warming up, we would walk around them to check the tires and look for rocks that might be lodged between the duallies. While I was inspecting my truck, the brakes released on their own, and it started rolling down the hill. I quickly ran alongside of it, jumped onto the running board, opened the door, entered the cab, and steered the truck down the hill to level ground, where it came to a stop. What I learned from this experience is that the moisture in the air tank would freeze overnight into a solid block of ice. This would give a false reading on the air pressure gauge indicating that the air pressure was full to capacity. Once the block of ice melted, the air pressure would drop below what was necessary to engage the brakes.

The next day the trucks were lined up again on a 20% incline, with brakes engaged. All the trucks were loaded with dirt in both chutes. My truck was parked near the bottom of the incline. There were three other trucks parked up the hill from me, all with their engines idling. The drivers were congregating outside their trucks visiting with each other. The black Mack truck, the newest in the fleet, started rolling down the hill, just like my truck did the day before. As employees, we were responsible for any damage to our rigs. If they broke down, we couldn't work. The driver of the black Mack truck was the most experienced driver within our fleet. He began chasing after it. He went to grab the handle to lift himself up onto the running board, but missed. He fell to the ground and got ran over by his truck, killing him instantly.

I was horrified! His eyes were opened and blood was pouring out of his nose. I had a whole new respect for the dangers of driving these big rigs. I got laid off some time later. I was trying to find my footing in the job market, and my wife Jean was doing the same. She took secretarial classes, and she eventually landed a good job at a hospital. We had two young children at that time. They were two and four years old. Whenever I searched for a job, my main motivation was how much it paid.

I worked a day job as a meat-packing laborer. It paid well and had good benefits for permanent, full-time employees. The only drawback was you had to work as a temporary on-call from a day hiring pool before they would consider you for full-time employment. I got hired because I was strong and capable of lifting heavy sides of beef. It was hard work and physically demanding, but I didn't mind because it kept me in shape, and made me stronger. I had to lift a quarter section of beef onto my shoulder, carry it onto a big refrigeration truck, and hang it on a hook.

One day, when I was working on the slaughter floor, a cow got loose, running in panic trying to escape. He was running through the blood-soaked floor from the other slaughtered cows. Can you imagine a 2,000 pound cow running loose in a slaughterhouse trying to avoid being killed? He skidded across the slippery floor trying to turn corners, looking for a way to escape. Running after him was a guy with a gun trying to shoot him. The shooter finally caught up to the cow and dropped him with two shots. They chained him up to the conveyor to finish processing him. That was quite a wild experience that I will never forget.

Work at the meat plant slowed, and they began laying off people, including me. My hiring days were becoming fewer and fewer, as I didn't have much seniority. It had been four years since I was discharged from the Army.

Enlightenment Begins

I learned that my GI Bill would cover any college courses that I wanted to take and give me a little extra money for expenses on the side. Jean was working a full-time job at the hospital, which provided steady income while I pursued an education.

It was an exciting time attending college. I felt so empowered and proud to be among other people seeking higher education. It was difficult for me to focus on any one particular degree to pursue. I was fascinated by everything, so I pursued a General Studies major. It seems I went from loving biology to anthropology and recreation to jewelry making. I finally graduated in 1978 with an Associate of Arts Degree.

I was encouraged by my teachers to continue my education in pursuit of a Bachelor's Degree at a University. Although that sounded exciting to me, it was scary to take on such a major challenge. Nevertheless, I felt that even if I failed trying, it still would be a positive, beneficial experience.

I enrolled in Metropolitan State University in Denver, Colorado. I pursued a major in Urban Studies and Sociology. My curriculum was grueling, but again I felt a great satisfaction being in this environment of higher education.

I started driving a taxicab at night in 1980, while attending college. It was good money and offered flexible hours that accommodated my school obligations. I would take care of our children during the day while my wife worked. This went on for years.

I enjoyed driving and meeting different people. Sometimes it was weird, scary and adventurous driving a cab. I was young and took advantage of opportunities without always thinking of the possible repercussions.

One night, while waiting outside of the bus station, a young couple entered my cab and said they wanted me to take them to a hotel. On the way to the hotel they asked if I would take them to New Orleans for Mardi Gras. I told them that I couldn't take them out of state in my cab, but I could do it in my own private car, and it would cost them $1,000. They agreed to the arrangement. So, I went home and told Jean that I was taking a trip out of town, and that I would be back in a few days.

The next day, I went back to the hotel to pick up the couple, and we immediately headed out of town. New Orleans was 1,300 miles southeast of Denver, and I was determined to get there and back as quickly as possible. The young man's name was Jason, age 27, and the young woman's name was Karen, age 24. We passed the time by talking about various things like music, partying, and drugs.

We stopped at a diner along highway 70 in Kansas to grab a meal. When Jason got up to use the restroom, Karen started leaning closer to me while she was talking, stroking my hand, and flirting with her eyes and smile. I could tell she wanted to have sex with me, and I wasn't quite sure how to handle the situation. She was really pretty, and I felt myself getting aroused.

We drove straight through to New Orleans and shared a hotel room to rest up before exploring the city. We ended up going to an oyster bar later that evening. Jason suggested I try oysters on a half shell. They didn't look too appealing to me at all. They looked slimy and reminded me of mucus. He told me that they taste great once you put hot sauce on them and swallow them whole. He demonstrated how to do it, and told me they were a great aphrodisiac, which would stimulate my sexual drive.

I decided to give it a try. I put the hot sauce on the oyster and swallowed it whole like he said, and it got stuck in my throat. I couldn't get it to come up or go down. I was gagging, and both of them were laughing at me. Finally, it slid down and I could breathe again. Then Jason said, "Now that you've done the first one, the rest will go down easier." I said, "No, thanks!"

Jason started hitting the booze pretty hard, so Karen and I took to the dance floor. We danced for quite a while when we heard a ruckus coming from the bar. Jason had become drunk and out of control. He began fighting with a few other guys at the bar. When the cops arrived, they looked at me and said, "You all ain't from around here are you? Get out of this bar or we'll take you to jail." We quickly guided Jason out of the bar and went back to our hotel room.

Jason wasn't content sitting around in a hotel room, so he left to go find a new bar. Karen and I were alone in the room and it wasn't long before she started coming on to me. She asked, "Will you sleep with me?" I was attracted to her, but I was also married. The thought of having sex with her was appealing, but it was also a risky move. I replied to her, "Sure, I'll sleep with you, but it will cost you." She paused, and smiled, and then said, "How much?" I answered, "One hundred dollars." She agreed, and we got busy before Jason came back from the bar.

Back in Denver on college campus, I loved seeing all the hot college girls. The good-looking bodies on campus made me want to shape up my body, so I took an elective class on bodybuilding. My body responded well to weight training. I made a lot of buddies in the weight training class. After weight training, we would go to the student union and drink beer, laugh and joke.

I soon grew to be 275 pounds of muscle mass. I was so big and strong that I took first place in the state novice power-lifting championship. My kids were so proud of me and even to this day talk about this accomplishment. My confidence in my physical ability grew, leading me to try out for the Denver Broncos Football Team. At the tryouts I had to perform running and jumping well. When I was running the 40-yard dash, I could hear coach Dan Reeves say, "Look at that big man go!" Although I didn't make the cut, I got a T-shirt and big thank-you from the Broncos. I continued to study hard and lift weights.

I took an internship at the Mennonite Urban Ministry as a grant writer. As such, it showed other aspects of urban planning. I made several visits to Denver City and County Planning Department. I was so fascinated by City Planning, I thought, "This is something I would love to do when I graduate."

In 1983, I graduated with a Bachelor's Degree in Urban Studies with a minor in Sociology. That was certainly a proud moment for me and my family. Although I hadn't found a job yet in any career capacity, the benefit of being a college graduate significantly changed my mindset. I felt smart, important, and relevant, and that boosted my confidence.

I continued driving a cab and occasionally a limousine, while looking for a career opportunity. While driving my cab, I would have intriguing conversations with business passengers. Perhaps someday, one of them would offer me a job lead. I had doctors, lawyers, engineers, judges, politicians, entertainers, and professional football players in my cab at one point in time. I loved learning and exchanging ideas about business with them and was intrigued by our conversations.

One day, a sharp-dressed black gentleman got into my cab at the Denver airport. I told him I was a recent college graduate and I was frustrated because I couldn't find a job in my field. He asked if I had ever considered graduate school to further my education. I said, "No, I haven't." I was tired of school and I just wanted a good job. He said the College of Design and Planning are looking for minority students for enrollment. He said having a B.A. Degree in Urban Studies is a good prerequisite to get in. He said to write the Dean of College and explain why you would make a good student for the program.

Thinking it through and talking with my wife, I weighed things out, and decided to write the Dean a letter. While waiting for a reply, I began to have self-doubt, because it was difficult enough getting my Bachelor's Degree; now I was going after a Master's Degree. It was surreal for me to even think I could achieve such a monumental task. About a week later, I received a letter from the Dean of Schools accepting me into the program. I was ecstatic and could not believe that this kid from Brooklyn was accepted into the postgraduate program.

The studies were tough and fascinating at the same time. I had different professors for each science, one for planning theory, economic planning, social and physical planning and statistical planning. I struggled quite a bit because I really didn't have the brainpower for Statistics, Methods and Techniques, Regression Analysis, Theory, etc. Even though I struggled, just being influenced by this level of thinking benefited me. Just having the opportunity to climb the higher educational ladder increased my knowledge and expanded my perspective, even though I was not the best student. That is what building character is all about.

My First Band

As I continued grad school, I rediscovered my true passion, which was singing. I hooked up with some musicians I met and started a band called "The Backseat Drivers." I was the lead singer and front man. Music and performing was so natural for me. I felt every note and thrived on connecting with my audiences. I was really good. We started getting regular gigs on weekends and were building a fan base.

I had difficulty retaining a good drummer. I settled for this guy who was an average drummer, but he had an attitude problem. We landed a regular gig at a bar near Washington Park, south of Denver. We had a packed night every weekend. I was constantly having to correct the drummer. Well, one weekend while gigging there, I couldn't believe it, but the drummer stopped playing to light a cigarette. At the conclusion of the show, I met with him outside the club. I told him that if he ever did that again I would fire him. He became hostile and it escalated into a fist fight. I dropped him to the ground like a rock. He was injured bad enough that the paramedics were called.

Thinking that the cops might take me to jail, I hightailed it home. I was very worried because of my past troubles with the law. When I got home, I told my family what had happened. My wife got some first aid ointment and applied it to my hand. I told everyone to be quiet as I closed all of the blinds and curtains to make it look like no one was home. After about an hour of pacing and peeping out the window to see if the cops were outside, I thought maybe if I called them to explain what happened, then maybe they would not arrest me.

I made the call and moments later two cops showed up at my door. I told them who I was and that I was in a bar fight earlier. They said they typically do not make arrest at bar fights unless it was more severe. They thanked me for calling them to report this incident and said goodnight. Boy, was I relieved since I was really trying to get my life on track and stay out of trouble.

The band was getting ever so popular. I befriended this guy named DJ. He could really play the trumpet well and he carried it everywhere he went. DJ asked if I wanted to go to a rock bar with him and we could sit in. I said, "Okay, that's cool." The feature band wasn't what I expected; it was raw heavy metal. I mean, these musicians looked like the band "Kiss." They wore tight leopard-skinned pants, big lion-style hairdos and six-inch boots. When they played their guitars, it made your teeth clinch and your hair blow from the sound waves.

I said to DJ, "Are you serious about sitting in with these guys?" He replied, "Jerry, you've got this! Have another drink and relax." I asked, "What song can we do with these guys?" He asked me, "What standard do you know that they can follow?" I replied, "Let's do 'Mustang Sally,' everybody knows that song." By the time we were called up to the stage, we had a lot of drinks and plenty of courage to perform with these big hair guys. The band introduced DJ and I as we stepped up to the stage that was about six feet above the floor below.

The crowd went wild as the lead guitarist ripped the melody, and I started singing, "Mustang Sally." DJ began blowing his horn really loudly to be heard above the amplified guitars. The audience erupted with cheers as the lead guitarist fell to his knees ripping out notes. DJ, not to be outdone, ran toward the front of the stage while blowing his horn, and leaped into the crowd. His landing was not so perfect. The crowd quickly moved out of his way, and he tumbled to the ground and rolled. It was an unbelievable sight to see. I laughed so hard, I almost lost my breath.

Job Hunting

I graduated with a Master's Degree in Land Use Planning in 1986. I practically levitated across the stage accepting my diploma. I was stoked beyond my wildest dreams. I could never have imagined that I would achieve a Master's Degree. I was so proud and elated.

I immediately began looking for jobs in the planning field. My search didn't land me any opportunities.

My younger brother, Pete, wanted to come and live in Denver near us. I was desperate for any kind of well-paying job at this point. I heard that the oil rigs in Wyoming were looking for workers and the pay was good. I told Pete about it and asked if he was interested in checking it out because he needed to find a job too. It sounded good, so we got in his car and he drove us to Medicine Bow, Wyoming. There were lots of cowboys and very few black people in Wyoming. We asked a local where the oil rigs were located, and he responded by pointing in the right direction, saying,"About ten miles."

We proceeded down a snow-covered dirt road. The farther we drove down the road, the more we realized it wasn't suitable for our kind of car. We needed a four-wheel drive. We were only two miles away from the oil rigs when the car wheels started spinning and we had to stop. We decided to walk the rest of the way. We approached the top of a large hill, and were astonished to see a field full of hundreds of cows separating us from the oil rig.

Pete proclaimed with apprehension, "I am not walking through that herd of cows, no way!" He had a look of fear on his face. I replied to him, "We've come too far to turn back now." I went on to say, "Besides, I don't see any bulls, and as long as we don't spook them, they probably won't stampede." He begrudgingly said, "Okay." Walking very quietly, we started to pass by the cattle. We drew the attention of some, but one in particular seemed to be getting agitated at our presence. It started to charge at us, and my brother shouted, "Oh shit!" We took off running as fast as we could to get to the other side. Fortunately, the cow stopped chasing us as we ran away from it. I think the reason it was agitated was because it had a calf nearby. She was just being protective.

As we approached the oil rig, the entire crew of rough-necks, including the foreman, couldn't believe their eyes, seeing two black men walking in the wilderness looking for a job. He was nice as he told us he wasn't hiring. He asked "Did you walk all the way from town"? I said, "No, we drove until our car got stuck and we walked from there." We told him about the cows and asked if he knew of another way we could walk back to our car without crossing that field. He smiled and said he would drive us back to our car. We certainly were delighted to accept his offer. As we drove through the town we saw a restaurant offering buffalo burgers. Never having had a buffalo burger before, he allowed us to stop and try them.

After returning to Denver, I was frustrated and did all I could to find a job. People were telling me I should apply in California, because that is where land use planners were in demand and hired. I began to put a plan together to look for work in California, because in those days the best way to get hired was to show up in person and hand them your résumé. So, I had this old van that I could sleep in and I had an acquaintance who lived in Pomona, California, who offered to help me.

My wife wasn't too keen on moving to California, but she knew how badly I wanted to work in the planning field with my degree. She also knew our marriage wasn't going so well and maybe a new place could get us on track. Besides, she wasn't happy with her job anyway. I headed for California, leaving her and the kids behind in Denver. I had enough money to last a month in Los Angeles.

I planned to take the southern route I-25 to I-40 into Gallup, New Mexico, and Flagstaff, Arizona. I thought this route would experience less snow and inclement weather, especially since my heater and defroster didn't work. The temperature was below freezing in Gallop and Flagstaff. I arrived in Flagstaff around 1 a.m. and I was cold. Being in my van was like being in a freezer. I thought maybe I would pull over at the rest stop and crawl in my sleeping bag to stay warm. All the cars parked at the rest stop looked eerily frozen and I didn't think after seeing that, it would be a good idea to sleep over there. There was danger of freezing or going into hyperthermia. I thought maybe I could warm up a little by going inside a gro-cery store. I stayed in the store until I warmed up. I asked the clerk how far it was to the warmer weather. She said Phoenix was about 60 miles south from Flagstaff. I climbed back in my van and drove like a bat out of hell trying to get to the heat. I soon felt the warmer climate with a sigh of great comfort.

I didn't waste any time once I got to L.A. I submitted appli-cations everywhere I could. I don't believe anyone experi-enced as much of L.A. as I did in 30 days. For the purpose of expediency, I drove to each municipality to submit an employ-ment application. I went to Rancho Palos Verde, a beautiful community with giant oceanside cliffs. I went to the cities of Paramount, Pomona, Glendale, Corona, and Palmdale, sub-mitting applications with no resulting interviews. I had mixed feelings about L.A. People didn't seem so friendly, and you really had to drive in lots of traffic to get anywhere. With money running low, I headed back to Denver. My family was glad to see me and I was glad to see them too. Although I was still disappointed, I didn't give up. I learned a lot through the process. I learned that most employers were seeking the top students. I was an average student, but I knew I could learn the job if I only had a chance.

Insight From the Author

Today I was listening to the news about five young black men who stole a lottery ticket truck. The police pursued them, shot and killed one of the men. The other four were taken into custody. I felt so bad for these young men. They thought if they had those boxes of lottery tickets they could cash in the winning tickets. They didn't realize that those tickets were null and void if not acquired legally. The reason I am sharing this story is there is a lot of senseless, uneducated, hopeless people out there committing acts of opportunity and desperation. I was one of those people in my youth. At this moment I wish I had a way to communicate to these young men and women, don't waste your life on material things that don't matter. Don't ruin your life by committing senseless crimes or hurting people. The true rewards in life come from respect, honor, morals and love for your fellow person. If you are self-destructive like I was, I know it is hard to see beyond the moment of selfish desires and motivations, but believe me because I was like you, life is so much more and so much better when you've embraced goodness.

What turned my life around was gaining knowledge and establishing a relationship with God. Learning takes time, but in time it will transform you. Do not conform to the ways of the world. Reach for the stars in heaven and embrace the Lord God Almighty. There is nothing greater than the love of God. Try him and you will see.

You may think joy and happiness comes from fast money, fast cars, sex, jewelry, sneakers, cellphones, etc. Those things may seem all that, but in the end, they leave you empty and unfulfilled.

People think that if they only had a million dollars..., In the Bible, God says he does not give us more than we can handle. He wants to know that we have the capability to manage money; and the disciplines that goes along with it. Many people have struck it rich through inheritance and even by winning multi-million lotteries and are broke a short time later. You might ask, why is that? Well, if they do not learn to earn their money, along with the disciplines of managing their money, then they tend to carelessly spend their money, squandering it away. I have learned that having character and relying on God for what he wants for me, is more valuable and sustainable than money alone. I realize that not everyone has that level of conviction or faith, but building character is where it starts.

My prayer, is that God will use my stories, and my past mistakes and experiences, to guide young, misguided youth to make better choices and avoid common pitfalls.

This chapter represents the roast beef of my wish sandwich, offering rich savory flavor, protein, nutrition, and long-lasting sustenance.

CHAPTER 7

Professional Life Begins

I received an internship at Douglas County Planning Department in Castle Rock, Colorado. I interned as a GIS mapping technician. Basically, I generated computerized land use maps. Working in a planning department gave me exposure to the entire functionality of what planners do in the real world. I worked there for a little over a year before my grant ran out. It was a small planning department undergoing budget constraints, so they didn't hire me. At least now I had experience in a specialized area of planning. I didn't think it would take long now to land a full-time job in Denver, but it just wasn't meant to be. I started looking at a professional Jobs Available publication listing jobs around the country. I started applying to places like Lansing, Michigan, Tampa, Florida, and Lake County, California. By the grace of God, I received an interview invite in Lake County, California. I was so excited! I wasn't going to pass this interview up for anything. The only problem was, we only had one car and Jean needed it to get to work.

I had a planner friend who said he had a car that he recently repossessed from a drug dealer who went to jail, and he would sell it to me for $500. He said it ran well and should get me to California and back with no problem. The car was definitely in good shape; however, it was pimped out. It was a Chrysler Cordoba with a leather-covered roof-top and back window. The rear window had a small circular porthole like you would see on a plane. The interior was plush red velvet with mood lights and a small chain-link steering wheel. It was black and dropped close to the ground. My friend and I were thinking that this car would be perfect in California, so I bought it. I decided to take my kids with me so they could see California. We headed out.

I wasn't sure what type of community Lake County offered. It turned out to be very rural, and I suspect it was also very conservative. My car seemed to be drawing a lot of attention, and some cops seemed to be tailing me as I drove through the area. When we arrived at the town of Lakeport, California, it was beautiful. The town sat on the shore of a huge lake called Clear Lake, which is one of the largest natural lakes in California, consisting of 125 miles of shoreline. My kids and I were excited to see so much outdoor nature, and loved the idea of going fishing in the lake. We instantly fell in love with this community.

I parked next to this four-story giant building. It was the biggest in the entire county. It was the county courthouse and administrative offices. I told my kids to wait in the car while I went in for the interview. When I exited the car, my kids said, "Daddy, why are all those people looking out the windows at us?" I looked up to see that every window, from the bottom to the top of the building, was full of people looking at us.

As I came out of the elevator on the fourth floor, I was greeted by a friendly receptionist. I took a seat while waiting for my interview. The director came out along with two other planners, and smiled at me while extending his hand. He said, "You must be Jerry." I replied, "How do you do?" He introduced himself, "I'm Alex, the planning director." He invited me back and I sat across the table from him and the two other gentlemen. Alex went on to say, "I gotta tell ya, Jerry. Anybody who can drive a car like yours, we gotta consider them for the job." They all laughed. I joined in the laughter, not really knowing what to think. It turns out my car made for quite an ice breaker.

The interview went well, at least from my perspective. The planning director said to me that he had many qualified finalists, and he should know where I was on the list by sometime tomorrow. I was instructed to call him when I got to Salt Lake City on my way back to Denver. I called him when I got to Salt

Lake City, and boy was I anxious. He told me that I was in the top three for consideration, and that one other candidate had a Ph.D. He instructed me to call him again when I got back to Denver. I hung up the phone with concern that I wasn't going to get the job offer.

We arrived back in Denver on Thursday. I was so excited and nervous when I made the phone call. The director told me, "I got some good news and some bad news. Which do you want first?" Naturally, I said the good news. He said, "You got the job." With excitement I yelled to my wife and kids, "I got the job! I got the job!" I regained my composure and thought to myself, what could the bad news be? So, I asked, "What is the bad news?" He then said, "You have to be back here to work by Monday morning at eight o'clock." I was so delighted to have a job in this beautiful community that I quickly said, "No problem, I'll be there!"

I borrowed some money from one of my buddies, and drove back to Lakeport, California, to start my new job. I shared a house with a planner who was also employed at the planning department. His main residence was in Chico, California. He would spend his weekends in Chico, and the work week sharing the house with me. We were not the most compatible roommates, but we tolerated one another. The house was next door to the county sheriff's residence. I heard from the neighbor across the street that when I moved in next door to him, the sheriff said to them, "There goes the neighborhood." I could only gather from his insinuation, that because I am black, I would somehow degrade the value, or threaten the peace and safety of the neighborhood. Of course, this is a common misperception of those who stereotype an entire race based upon a few individuals' bad behavior. Unfortunately, this was not going to be the only time I would experience racial bias in this predominately white, Northern California community.

I am not implying that the actions of some, mean the entire community is tainted. People should be treated as individuals, and any judgement that takes place should be based upon the content of their character and behavior alone. Nothing else. If everyone exhibits the same behavioral traits, should race or ethnicity even matter? Racism is something that is taught and learned. It is difficult to change the mindset of someone who believes so earnestly that their viewpoint of any particular race is skewed. I know I have struggled with my own racism towards white people from early childhood.

Months later, my wife thought it best that I bring the kids to California to live with me and start school in the fall. She said she would join us later. I agreed, so I rented a two-bedroom apartment in Lakeport prior to driving back to Colorado to pick them up.

The kids were excited to relocate to California with me. We rented a small U-Haul truck to take some of the essentials, and hooked up my car to the backside in tow. We said good-bye to their mother and began our journey west. As we drove through Wyoming, we hit a late spring snowstorm. It was treacherous driving. Visibility was so poor that I could barely tell where the road was. A big rig passed us on the right and projected a large ice rock that hit our windshield and broke the passenger side wiper.

There was no place to pull over to wait out the storm or get roadside assistance. I had to keep driving. My kids were getting scared, especially because it was hard to see the road. I moved over to the right lane and did my best to follow the truck's tire tracks. That was scary, because I had to travel at a high rate of speed in order to avoid being rear-ended by one of those big rigs. My daughter had to roll down her window to clear the ice and snow from the windshield as we plowed down the road. Eventually, we made it to Evanston, Wyoming, where I bought windshield wiper blades. We continued our journey to California without further incident.

Single Dad Blues

I enrolled the kids in Lakeport Middle and High School begin-ning in the fall. We were walking along Lakeport's main street one day, when a car full of people yelled racial slurs at us as they drove by. I told my kids not to worry, some people don't know that things they say can be misinterpreted and seem hateful. That was just the first of many questionable treat-ments my kids received.

After enduring racial prejudice from both students and teacher faculty for over a year, I took my grievances to the principal and suggested that the teachers and students should be made aware of their offensive language. He told me that if I had a problem with the school, I should take my kids somewhere else. So, I did. I enrolled them into Kelseyville High School, about 10 miles away.

It seemed in our best interest to move to Kelseyville, which was more multi-culturally populated. We found a four-bed-room house to rent near the state park that had a beautiful creek running through it.

My kids and I traveled a lot together. I took them to muse-ums and all kinds of events. We loved hanging out together. One afternoon, I took them with me to a pet store in Lakeport. As we entered the store, we were greeted by a giant cockatoo perched freely on a limb above a table. The bird whistled at us to come over and visit. We were curious, so we went over to check him out. I suggested to my kids that they stick their hand out because the bird was extending his leg out like he wanted to perch on someone's arm.

Both kids adamantly declined the invite. So, I said, "What's the matter? Are you scared?" They said, "No, dad." "Let me show you how it's done," I confidently proclaimed. My son said, "Dad, I wouldn't do that if I were you." I proceeded to extend my hand out, and the bird, named Charlie, perched himself on my hand. When I tried to get Charlie to step back onto his branch, he began to walk up my arm toward my head. So, I leaned forward trying to get him to come down, but then he started pecking at my ear. I began to sweat profusely. I yelled at my kids to get him off. They said "Uh-uh Dad, we told you not to pick that bird up." The pet shop owner came to rescue Charlie because I began to threaten to swat the feathers off Charlie if somebody didn't get him. The owner calmly said, "Now, now Charlie, I see you got another one." My kids and I still laugh until we cry about that bird story.

I started attending some local jam sessions at different people's houses in Lakeport. This is how I met my soon-to-be band members. They had heard about my singing ability from people who I played with at jam nights. Some of the locals had heard that I was interested in starting up a band again, and they recommended that I try to recruit of few local blues musicians, who were quite good. Once we met, we joined together as musicians very quickly. Together we became known as "Blu Heyz."

Once word got out that we were a hot band with a kick-ass lead singer, we made all kind of headlines in the local paper.

Both kids excelled in sports, taking Kelseyville to multiple football, basketball and volleyball state championships. It felt good to see my kids thrive in school and sports, and squash our competitor, Lakeport, at every turn.

My son's biggest highlight, although there were many, was when he was awarded the MVP at a college bowl game where they won as underdogs. I was so proud of him. Unfortunately, I had a gig that I had to perform about 200 miles north of where the game was being played. I got to see most of the game before I had to leave, and my son was playing like he was in the zone. He could not be stopped, even when the other team would put multiple blockers against him. My son would not be denied and kept that quarterback on his back, sack after sack. He called from his hotel room after the game to tell me they won the championship and he received the MVP defensive award. He was jazzed out of his mind, as I could hear his teammates in the background, hooting and yelling with elation. I was so excited for him, I announced it over the microphone prior to starting the next set.

I was privileged to sing the national anthem at my son's football games because I had become a popular singer in the community. After the anthem, the crowd would erupt with appreciation. It was such a wonderful patriotic feeling. I was so proud of my son. He played like a champion every time he got on the field.

My daughter was a standout in her own right. She won the state basketball championship as well as receiving the top player status in the state. She was a physical, inside player. She was hard to stop from scoring or rebounding.

During one of my wife's visits, she and I went to support our daughter at a regional girls' basketball game in Fallon, Nevada. My daughter was playing very physical and aggressive, like she always does. The girls on the other team were playing aggressive too, cutting her and scratching her all throughout the game. My daughter would dribble the ball while position-ing her body between the ball and the defenders. She was quick and precise with her pivots, and successfully scored many shots to the basket.

The other team had fans and family members in the stands that didn't like how physical and aggressive my daughter was playing. Some of them began shouting offensive slurs at her. In defense of my daughter, our fans and I began yelling back in support of her. One of the parents from the other team called my daughter the N-word, and that really upset my wife. She yelled to the parent that these were kids, and there is no place for that language. Then a male member of their family stood up and yelled some profanities back at my wife. I instantly got involved in the melee and told him he'd better sit his fat ass down or I would kick it. The principal had to break it up and we were escorted out of town. My daughter's team won the game.

A co-worker had a boat for sale that needed some work. I thought it was a great buy and an opportunity for me to own my own boat. It took me and my friend two months to get it rebuilt and running. I took it out on the lake often. I even took my brother Butch out for a ride when he would visit. He was scared the entire time, especially when I banked it hard. He would yell, "Stop playing around, Jerry! You're always playing around!" He remembered from our childhood how much of a daredevil I was. I would take my dad for a ride when he visited, and he just loved it.

Sink Or Swim

As our children were finishing high school, my wife and I decided to divorce. It was mutual and uncontested. We both realized that our lives were different, and now that the children were moving on to college, it was the right time to go our separate ways. We stayed in the house we rented in Lakeport, and I moved out a couple of months later when I finished construction of my new single-family home. We had been married for twenty-four years.

My son left to attend college at the University of Nevada in Reno. He told his mother that she could join him once he got settled. My daughter, while attending Shasta Community College, received a full scholarship to play basketball at Abilene Christian University in Texas. My wife and I remained friendly toward one another, and together we helped get our daughter settled at ACU.

One Memorial Day weekend, while my daughter was visiting from college, I thought it would be nice to take her out on the lake in my boat. This particular weekend also happened to be a very busy bass tournament weekend. I decided to finally get the boat insured on the Friday before the big weekend, just in case anything were to happen.

On Saturday, we packed a lunch and hopped into the boat. While backing out from the boat dock, a cable link broke and the throttle and steering wheel locked up, and the boat accelerated in reverse. I was trying franticly to unlock the steering wheel and slow the boat down. I was not paying much attention to the direction the boat was taking. My daughter yelled, "Watch out!" because the boat had circled backed toward the dock where other boats were parked.

Before I could shut the engine down, the back of my boat rammed into a beautiful $30,000 bass boat parked at the pier. The impact was so hard, from my boat being a heavy weighted tri-hull boat, that it totally destroyed that beautiful bass boat. I was horrified and embarrassed, and by then a ton of onlookers had come over to witness this debacle.

The owner of the bass boat came running over to see what happened to his boat. I apologized profusely and explained the mechanical malfunction that I had. I also gave him my insurance card. The following business day I called my insurance agent who was not too happy about my accident. He could not believe that in less than 48 hours, I cost his insurance company $30,000. I said, "Sorry, but that is what insurance is for." He canceled my policy and it was difficult finding boat insurance after that.

Months later, on a beautiful fall day, I decided to take the boat out for one last cruise before winterizing it for the season. It was about 90 degrees and I was in shorts and a tank top. As I was cruising around the lake I unexpectedly ran out of gas. The tank read one quarter full. Well, obviously, that was a false reading. I was stranded, just floating on the middle of the lake, which had approximately 125 miles of shoreline. I figured someone was bound to come by and help me out.

Well, hours passed, and evening was approaching. I began to get anxious as the sun started descending below the horizon.

Now, in a mountainous climate when the sun goes down, it gets cold, especially on a clear night. As darkness came, I had my doubts if anyone could find me, since I had no lights. I was getting overly concerned that without a blanket, I could get hypothermia. I had to stay warm if I was going to survive the night. I was getting desperately cold, so I pulled up the carpet from the boat floor and rolled myself up in it. It worked! I fell asleep while my boat rocked slightly on the dark water.

I woke up once in the night to pee over the side of the boat. It was freezing cold! As I laid back down, all tucked into my carpet, I wondered if any of my friends would miss me enough to call the sheriff. Only a few of them knew I took the boat out that day.

I woke up much later to the sound of diesel trucks roaring on the roadway. I jumped to my feet to get my bearings. I had drifted over to the east shoreline adjacent to Hwy 20. I was about 50 yards from the shore. The water was pushing me in that direction, so I used my hands to help paddle me in. Boy was I glad to be on land!! Leaving my boat beached on shore, I started walking down the highway and tried to wave down a sheriff as he drove right by me. I walked about a mile when I found a phone booth to call 911. As I was calling, to my surprise, my son and ex-wife showed up. They said they got a call from my friend who said I was missing on the lake. My ex-wife jokingly said, "I was coming to find you to see if you were dead so I could collect on the life insurance." I was glad to see them, and it was around 5 a.m. when I got back home. They drove back to Reno after determining that I was safe and sound.

I loved boating and grew more confident taking it out on the lake. I used to take it out at night to different bars around the lake. It was really beautiful cruising the lake under the star-filled sky. I could clearly see the Milky Way, the Big and Little Dipper, the planet Venus, which was bright like a star, and the occasional shooting star or meteorite.

There was a soul band playing at a venue along the lake that I thought would be fun to attend. I had an extra ticket, but I didn't have anyone to go with me. My white neighbor, who was a former biker, seemed pretty cool, even though I didn't know him very well. I thought he might like blues music, so I asked him if he would like to go, and he said yes.

We took my boat and cruised across the lake to the bar. I bought him a few drinks and introduced him to some of my friends. We got separated, so I began to mingle with the crowd. A lot people there knew me because of my musical popularity. I was having a pretty good time until a group of angry black musicians approached me about my guest. Apparently, my neighbor was calling these black men "Niggers" and telling them he was a friend of mine. I didn't know if my neighbor was actually racist or just dead drunk. In any event, we were about to get our asses kicked, when the security guard asked us to leave.

I escorted my neighbor down to the boat dock and told him if he continued his vulgar language, he would need to find another way home. I suggested he sit in the boat and calm down, which he did. While standing on the dock this young lady came over and began flirting with me. She asked if I would take her for a boat ride, and I said sure. It was a beautiful summer night, as I drove the boat out into the lake. I shut off the engine and we continued conversating. My neighbor started scaring the girl by suggesting we rape her. I was thinking to myself, "What the hell, dude?" She began to panic, and said, "Please don't hurt me!" I reassured her that nobody was going to touch her, and I started the boat to take her back to shore. My drunken, idiot neighbor continued his threats toward her. I told him, "If you don't shut the f*** up, you'll be swimming home, because I will throw you overboard!"

I got the young lady back to the dock where the bar was. She gave me an endearing hug and a peck on the cheek and said, "Thank you." I took that idiot back home and that was the last time I would have any interaction with him, even though he later apologized.

This incident pounded home to me the importance of hanging out with people of good character. I didn't know this guy had issues like that, but if he had hurt that girl, I would have been just as guilty as him for simply being in the same vicinity. They call it guilty by association.

I was impressed with how I handled that dude, considering my younger self probably would have entertained the idea of taking advantage of such a pretty girl. This was a sign that I had matured quite a bit, and I was proud of who I was becoming.

Local Fame

My band was hired to do a show in a nearby community called Cobb Mountain. The resort we were playing at was hosting a biker party. Motorcycle groups gathered there from all over the region to party. There were also a bunch of rowdy college kids there too.

We were playing some good blues music when a big fight broke out between the college kids and the bikers. Tables and chairs, punches and people started flying. We stopped playing music and one of the bikers told us to keep playing through the fight. It was like a scene from a movie. After the fight, the bikers paid for all the broken equipment.

I invited my dad to come out and visit me and the kids in Lakeport. My dad was really proud of my musical talent. He felt really important and proud when I would introduce him as my father at my shows. I was playing at a bar called the Flamingo, along the shores of Clear Lake. My dad was having a good time, he just danced and danced. My dad was always a good dancer. That is probably where I got my rhythm from. My dad was in his seventies, but you couldn't tell it, because he was energetic and youthful looking.

He sure liked women. He was slow dancing with this beautiful young blond, in her late twenties. He held her tight as they slow danced to a ballad that I was singing. My dad's signature moves were this herky-jerky motion when he danced. It was just too funny. After that slow dance he was in love. He told me later that he hadn't had a boner like that in twenty years. We laughed about that for a long time.

Our band was getting good reviews and gaining notoriety. We were hired for summer park concerts and gigs all along the north coast. In Lakeport, Octoberfest was a popular event and thousands of people would come from all over, even surrounding states. We were hired as the showcase band. It was exhilarating. My son came from Reno with his girlfriend and cheered from the front row.

My son had seen me on stage before and he wasn't too surprised by my performances. His girlfriend, however, thought she had met a superstar. The crowd of thousands roared with approval as they danced in the streets. My stage presence as the lead singer was infectious. I would dance and strut across the stage, making eye contact with everyone. It was on!

In fact, I often experienced women throwing their undergarments at me while preforming, and sometimes, women would jump on stage and begin grinding their hips next to me. There was this one time a hot, sexy, scantily dressed, beautiful young woman jumped onto the stage and started dancing very erotic and seductive with me. She was wearing a tight, low-cut, shimmery miniskirt. While performing, I could feel her warm, seductive breath as she came closer, inviting me to engage with her. Her hips were swaying to the music, and her braless breasts mesmerized me, as they danced around in her blouse. I tried to dance away from this seductress, but she wouldn't let me go. It was difficult not to engage her because dancing with her was like having sex. The crowd and band members cheered me on to dance with her.

Our band, Blu Heyz, made the front page of the local community newspaper. We became so popular that we started opening shows for major artists.

Opening for the Temptations was the highlight of my musical career. When we got the call that we were the opening band for the Temptations, it made us all feel that we were on the edge of bigger and greater things. We were stoked and it instantly elevated our confidence.

The Temptations' show was at the Konocti Harbor Inn, located on the shores of beautiful Clear Lake, California. The sound system at this facility was top of the line. As we prepared the sound check, we felt so amazing, like superstars. We performed what is called the "dinner set." Dining tables filled the room as people were enjoying their meal before the main show.

Our first song was "Tell It Like It Is" by the Neville Brothers. My band was tight as they came in together with the musical intro prior to my singing. The sound was excellent. I came in singing, "If you want... something to play with...." Instantly all eyes and ears focused on the stage. I was in rare form as I strutted across the stage, engaging the audience, especially the beautiful women. I dropped to my knees onstage, in front of a woman sitting at the table. She screamed with excitement as I sang the phrase of the song, "Don't play with my heart if you are not serious." The audience went wild with applause and stood to their feet. Our performance was so good that the Temptations came out of their dressing room to see what the excitement was all about.

After our performance, the Temptations took the stage. You could tell our show got the crowd excited and ready for more. The Temptations started inviting people from the audience to come up on stage and participate with them. My son, being in the front row, told the bouncer, "Man, my dad loves the Temptations. You just gotta let him get up on stage with them." The bouncer said, "Ya, okay. I'll call him up."

When he called me up on stage, the Temptations said, "Can you dance?" I quickly replied with a smile, "Ya, I can dance. I can sing too!" They responded saying, "Oh ya? Let me see you dance." So, I started dancing. Then they said, "Now let me see you sing!" I took the microphone the lead singer and began singing, "I know you want to leave me... but I refuse to let you go!" Their eyes got big and they tilted their heads in disbelief. I went on to sing, "If I have to beg, plead for your sympathy... I don't mind 'cause you mean that much to me... I ain't too proud to beg...." As I began singing the chorus, to my surprise, all of the Temptations came in and sang background vocals, "Whoot, whoo."

What an incredible moment! A friend of mine captured the perfect photo of me singing with the Temptations. It was amazing!

At the same venue, my band was hired to open for the King of Blues, B.B. King. When it was B.B. King's stage, he came out giving us much recognition and kudos, saying to his audience, "how about that Blu Heyz Band?" I also have a band photo with B.B. King in the middle. We went on to open for other big names, such as, The Starship, David Lindley, Little Charlie and the Night Cats, and The Ford Brothers. We even became the marquee New Year's Eve band at Konocti Harbor Inn. We were hired for many special events and concerts in the park.

God, Are You Still Here?

I wasn't feeling very well for a while, so I decided to go see my doctor. My oldest brother Bubby had recently passed away from a massive heart attack at age 50. Once my doctor learned about my brother's untimely death, he thought it would be wise to do a heart examination on me. He ordered a heart echo scan, and nothing of concern showed up. My cardiologist was very thorough and ordered one more additional test called an angiogram. The procedure seemed evasive as it required a catheter inserted in the main artery of my inner upper thigh. The blood flow takes this microscopic camera into the heart chamber where a dye is released. I was awake during the procedure, and the doctor pointed to the screen and said, "See this, Jerry?" as he pointed to monitor. I said, "Yeah, what are those squiggly lines, and what are the spaces that are blank?" He calmly said, "Those are blockages. You need open heart surgery, and we should do it tomorrow."

I sat there stunned. I couldn't believe what I was hearing. I said to the doctor, "Man, I just saw this surgery on the Discovery Channel. I want a second opinion." My doctor went out and came back in with a heart surgeon. He took a look at my results and agreed that the best course of action would be to open up those arteries as soon as possible to avoid a major heart attack. They went on to explain the procedure to me. They said they would have to stop my heart and place me on a pump until they repaired the arteries.

I told them that I wasn't really feeling all that bad, and maybe I should leave, and just see how it . They said, "Hey Jerry, we know you are a singer, and you have a full life. We know you're also a planner for our community, so we see you as valuable. We ain't gonna let you die, man. Let me give you something to relax you."

I was scared out my wits! The possibility of death was staring me in the face. There was an 80% chance that I was going to be okay, but all I could focus on was that 20% chance of death or of something going completely wrong.

In preparation for the procedure, I was instructed to thoroughly wash the area down the center of my chest and both inner calves with iodine. The calves were where they would extract the veins to repair the arteries to my heart. As I washed, I began sobbing because I was scared of dying.

It seemed like only a few minutes passed after the four-hour surgery was completed. I heard a voice calling my name, "Jerry, Jerry, it's time to wake up." The voice of a female nurse so sweetly said, "The surgery was a success," as I opened my eyes. I was rolled away to ICU where I spent the first couple of nights. They got me out of bed immediately after surgery to sit me up in a chair. My chest was bandaged like a mummy, but I felt no pain.

My son and his college buddy were my first visitors. The nurse came in while they were there and instructed me to blow into a tube to lift the ping pong ball within it. They wanted me to blow hard enough to levitate the ping pong ball within the chamber. I thought that this would be easy enough, but my son and his friend laughed because no matter how hard I blew, the ping pong ball stood motionless. The nurse said the exercise was important and necessary to prevent the pneumonia bacteria from developing in my lungs. Blowing into the tube also helped to strengthen my lungs.

Coughing was a painful result from the blowing, which explained my reluctance to blow harder into the tube. It hurt when I coughed; it felt like the stitches holding my chest together were going to come apart. They gave me a pillow that I later named "Snuggles." It was an important part of my healing process. I would hold Snuggles tight against my chest when I coughed, to give me counterpressure support. It helped keep my chest from feeling like it was ripping open.

The next day they wanted me to stand and then walk. The idea behind this was to get me moving and actively exercising as soon as possible. I heard some familiar voices in the hall coming toward my room, and I broke out singing, "The Boys Are Back in Town." My band members entered my room with bright eyes and big smiles when they heard me singing. "You just had open heart surgery and you're already singing dude?" They were happy to see that I was going to be alright, and I was happy to have good friends that would come visit me in the hospital.

Five days after the surgery I was being discharged. Because I had no one at home to help me, I was resistant and frankly emotional at the idea of leaving the security of the hospital so soon. My ex-wife volunteered to help me. She assured me she would take care of me. The doctor instructed me to take it easy when I got home. When we arrived back at my house in the mid-afternoon, I felt great, I mean really great. That same day, the concrete crew that I had previously hired, showed up to pour an RV driveway at my house. I decided to go out and help them. I didn't feel so good after that. Everything was hurting.

At times, the pain was excruciating during the healing period. The pain medication the doctors gave me wasn't really working. I remember suffering in agony one night while watching the Christian channel. I called them for prayer. I said to them, "Please pray for my pain, because I just had open heart surgery." On television while I was watching, they began to pray for me, and it was comforting.

I called the doctor to complain that the pain medication was ineffective. He had no advice on what to do, because he felt that they had prescribed me the strongest pain medication that should have been adequate to treat the pain. I took matters into my own hands and started taking over-the-counter pain relief medication such as Excedrin, Tylenol, and Advil. I rotated these three drugs every four hours which gave me relief.

Recovery was slow, extremely painful, and difficult. My chest and sternum, where they cracked my chest open, was being held together by some wire and stiches. This incision area is commonly referred to as "The Zipper." My chest wound hurt so badly, especially when I coughed, or tried to lie down in a prone position. So, I slept in a recliner chair for three months, which added to my discomfort. Each day I would extend my walk a little farther and eventually got up to walking five miles a day. I bought a bike and rode it for miles as well. I lost a lot of weight and was in great shape by the time I went back to work.

So High

I got back into the music scene with my band, and we continued to play all over northern California. We used to play at this hole-in-the-wall bar in Humboldt County, California. It was probably 200 miles or so from Lake County. We did weekend shows there, which were a lot of fun. The crowd was mostly hippies and bikers. After a show I would often get invited to stay at different folks' homes. One night, after a show, we were invited over to this girl's house to smoke some marijuana. I was expecting her to break out a baggie full of weed, but she drug out a large trash bag full of weed. I started laughing. I had never seen so much marijuana.

Another time I was invited over to someone's home, and they offered me some cake. The cake tasted so rich and buttery. I ate the first piece and then was offered more. I ate another piece and the host's boyfriend said, "Did you tell him what was in the cake?" I said excitedly, "Yeah, what's in it?" She said, "It's 'ganja' cake." I asked, "What is 'ganja' cake?" She said it's made with marijuana butter.

I noticed I was feeling higher and higher, and it made me start to panic. I felt like I was having shortness of breath. I quickly got in my van and drove erratically to the grocery store five miles away in town. I asked the grocer when I arrived where they kept the nasal inhalers to help me breathe. I started breathing the vapors in, but I was still feeling higher, and seemed like I was going to black out. I asked the grocery clerk where the hospital was. He said it was around the block. I pulled up to the emergency entrance, debating if I should go in. I was embarrassed. A male hospital attendant came over to me in my van and asked if I was okay. Still in a state of panic, I said to him, "I think I ate some marijuana cake, can you help me?" He said, "You must be a flat lander, because every now and then we see cases like yours from people in the flat lands."

He helped me out of the van and sat me on a bench in the emergency room. I asked him if there was something that they could administer that would bring me down. He said the only thing they could do was monitor me. He said, "Just sit here and I will check on you in a bit." As I lay on the bench, I felt like I was in a twilight zone. I could hear the intercom calling, "Dr. so and so, code blue." After lying there for a while, I started feeling really good, so I got ready to leave and the nurse attendant said, "You must be feeling better? You don't look gray anymore." I said, "I feel good, like James Brown. I'm going home." He said, "Okay, drive careful." I drove all the way home, 200 miles. I was having periodic relapses, so when I got home, I was paranoid. I closed the curtain, locked the door, and went to sleep.

This chapter represents the pepper jack cheese of my wish sandwich. Hot and fiery while being deeply satisfying.

CHAPTER 8

Single and Shackled

I was approached by a City Councilman to consider taking a planning job in his town, across the lake. I was bored with my current situation and figured this new job might provide the diversity I was longing for, so I took the job. I sold my home in Lakeport and moved to the City of Clearlake. I rented a small cottage on the lakefront that had its own boat dock. It had a 10-foot security gate in the front yard adjacent to the street.

At this time, Clearlake was a depressed city. It had a lot of abandoned buildings and properties. The community was overrun with poverty, crime, drugs, and alcohol addiction. A large percentage of the population was on welfare and/or Social Security dependent.

I didn't fit too well into this community. It appeared that the police department in Clearlake was even more racially biased toward black people than what I experienced in Lakeport. As a city planner, I worked in the same building as the police officers. I was the only black employee for the entire city at that time.

One summer evening, I was riding my bicycle with my headphones on, along the main street that circled the lake. A police officer came up behind me and turned on his emergency lights. I pulled over to the side of the road to let him by, and he followed me. He got out of his car and approached me saying, "You're not supposed to have headphones on while riding your bike." I replied, "No problem, I won't wear them anymore." He immediately demanded, "Let me see your driver's license!" Since when do you need to have a driver's license to ride a bike? He continued to harass me as I tried to explain to him I worked for city too. He finally let me go, but I was totally upset at the way he treated me and thought, "I will report him to the chief." I spoke with the chief the next day about the incident and told him I thought it was racially motivated. He spoke with the officer and I received an apology.

Living on the lake had its benefits. I would often sit in my living room and look out the picture window, and watch the water ripple from the boats passing by, or from the slight evening breeze. A big oak tree limb also hung in the view of my window. At night, a family of raccoons would gather on the limb, and peer into my living room. They seemed to enjoy my company. It was nice to imagine that these new furry friends were accepting of someone that obviously looked different from them, into their own environment.

While sleeping one night, a banging sound came from under the floor in my bedroom. It woke me up. It was followed by a loud, "eek eek eek," sound, and then a pungent odor permeated the room. The odor was so strong it began burning my eyes. I jumped out of bed and ran outside while gasping for fresh air. A group of skunks had taken residence under my cottage.

Unfortunately, this was not an isolated incidence. This happened night after night for an entire week. "Eek, eek eek!" sounds followed by intense odors that made my eyes bleed. The skunks were having an orgy and it didn't appear as though they planned on leaving anytime soon. Either they needed to go, or I needed to go.

I called the Department of Fish and Game to come and remove these smelly sex addicts from under my house. I was made aware that the entire region was experiencing a skunk problem, and the trapper would be unavailable for months. The man on the phone said, "You can get rid of them yourself by getting a trap from the feed store." I replied, "And then what do I do with them?" He answered, "That is what you need to figure out." I grabbed my keys and headed off to the feed store to get a trap.

The feed store clerk said the best bait for skunks is peanut butter and yogurt. He told me to tie a long rope to the cage so I would not get sprayed from the skunk. I opened the trapdoor and placed the bait on the tray that releases the trapdoor once the bait has been taken. That evening, I placed the trap cage near the entrance where the skunks got under my house. About half an hour later, I heard the trapdoor shut. I hurried outside to see a skunk milling around in the cage. I was so elated! I was one skunk closer to getting a good night's sleep.

The plan was to grab the ten-foot rope from the pier and drag the cage, with the skunk in it, toward the lake and submerge it under water until the skunk succumbed. Bubbles started coming up from the submerged cage. I wasn't taking any chances. I tried pulling the cage into deeper water, but the force of the water opened the trap door. I didn't realize skunks were such good swimmers.

As the skunk was swimming its way back to land, I panicked and ran to grab a shovel at the edge of the pier. I swung at the soaked, half-dazed creature and missed. I quickly darted and swung again, hoping it couldn't spray a moving target. Missing again and again, the little varmint waddled its way to refuge under the house. I was totally frustrated, hoping the skunk had a short memory. I didn't want it to communicate to the other skunks what had happened after having a tasty meal. I wondered if maybe the skunk would think it was all a bad dream.

Ultimately, the power of peanut butter and yogurt was irresistible. Over the next few days, I was able to capture all of the skunks living under my house. I boarded up the hole, and I slept fragrance-free from then on.

A few months later, I heard a knock on my door. I opened the door to a cute blonde who said she had been wanting to meet me because she heard about my band. She asked if she could come in. We ended up talking for hours. She was funny and I enjoyed her company. As she was leaving, she turned to me and asked, "Is it alright if I come over later for a drink?" I said, "That would be cool. Come on over." I was single and lonely. She came back that evening. We had a drink which led to many drinks. We had sex and she stayed with me all night.

I found out later that the local Indian community called this cute blonde Lunar Eclipse. So, for this story's sake, I will refer to her as Lunar.

Lunar and I quickly became a couple, and we started doing more things together. I soon learned that Lunar was an alcoholic and bipolar, a mentally unbalanced disorder. I took her to one of my performances and she tried to beat up another girl that was hitting on me after the show.

It turns out she came from a line of drug addicts and alcoholics. I'd never been in a relationship with an addict before, and I didn't really understand the dysfunctionality that comes along with it. I wasn't innocent in this messy relationship, because I was codependent and addicted to sex.

In a small town like Clearlake, it was nearly impossible to keep my relationship with Lunar private. My employer and coworkers at the city knew that I was dating the town drunk.

One night, Lunar showed up at my home drunk and agitated. I didn't want to let her in, so I joined her on the street in front of my house. She picked up a stick and swung it at me, and I blocked it with my arm. The stick broke upon impact. I told her, "Calm down or I'm going to call the police!" She picked up a rock and tried to smash my head with it. I darted away and began dialing 911 on my cell phone. She begged me not to call the police and promised to calm down. So, I hung up the phone.

She calmed down and asked if she could use the bathroom. She was in there for a long time. I went in to check on her and found her slicing her wrist. I grabbed her hand and took the razor blade away from her. She sobbed as I bandaged her wrist. I was able to calm her again, and we sat on the porch and talked.

A city police officer pulled up to the house and asked if everything was alright. I said everything was fine. He asked me if I called 911 from my house. I said "No," which wasn't a lie, because I called from the street, not my house. This was the same racially biased officer that previously demanded I show him my driver's license while riding my bicycle. News traveled, and I ended up getting fired from the city for lying to an officer.

I needed to get the heck out of this bumpkinville community and find a place more progressive. My son lived in Reno, Nevada, so I thought that might be a good place for us to try to get a fresh start. Lunar and I moved into a small, one-bedroom apartment in Reno, Nevada.

It turns out you can't escape chaos when you bring it with you. Reno is a gambling town. Casinos offered their patrons free drinks as long as you were gambling. Lunar would take people's drinks when they weren't looking. She got kicked out of multiple casinos for this behavior. She was in and out of detox centers on a regular basis.

I found some serenity in rollerblading around the local man-made marina. It had a three-mile-long circular path that encompassed the lake. I skated the marina every day for hours. My life was a mess. I needed clarity. I needed to heal from the trauma of losing my job. I just kept skating every day for an entire year until money ran out.

God worked through my children to get to me. When they were very young, they had a wonderful, loving grandma who took them to church whenever they would visit her in Colorado Springs. My children have been blessed with the knowledge of Christ throughout their lives. When I moved to Reno, my son invited me to his church, where I went from a walk, to a full-on sprint, into the arms of Jesus. I had experienced the Gospel intermittently throughout my life. But my children paved the way for me by their faith. Their example led me to my breakthrough with God, and the fulfilling relationship I now have with Him. They helped me to open up and showed me what it is to love God. Nothing can ever separate us from God's love. God's love is infinite!

The End of Madness

As my relationship with God grew, I felt directed to attend a church that was known for helping people overcome addiction. I figured this would be good place for Lunar to connect. This new church quickly adopted me into their worship team, which I loved being a part of. The church also offered a prayer room that we could use any time we needed.

I found peace and healing power in prayer. So, I would leave work on my lunch hour and head for the prayer room, where I would get on my knees and pray for up to 45 minutes. Praying like this was something I learned from my former church. We would gather at six in the morning and pray for an hour together. I learned from this experience that prayer is powerful, and God hears our prayers, even when we may think he doesn't.

Alcoholism is a powerful addiction that many people have difficulty overcoming. But God is more powerful than anything. Even Alcoholics Anonymous knows that, because they encourage people with addictions in their program to tap into their higher power. We know the higher power is God even though they avoid using His name. However, in their serenity prayer, it starts by saying, "God please grant me the wisdom...." My point is that God is the way, and He is the answer.

Lunar felt empowered through prayer too. The congregation really focused on supporting her sobriety and praying over her on a regular basis. I could see that she was making progress.

A few months later, Lunar had learned that her sister, who ran off to Texas with a drug dealer, was found beaten to death in a motel room in El Paso, Texas. It was tragic, because the family was destitute and could not afford to bring her body back to California for burial. She was only 26 years old. I attended a small memorial service the family held at the Clearlake City Park with Lunar. Tragedy struck this family like a ton of bricks. The oldest sister, who was married to an addict and had three children, was hit by a drunk driver and hospitalized, and in a coma for three months.

Of course, these tragedies weighed heavily on Lunar, and made it even more difficult for her to overcome her addictions. She was truly losing her mind, but I tried to help her, only to learn that I was enabling her by being codependent. She tried to overcome her addictions by attending AA meetings and accompanying me to church on weekends.

I landed a great job as an Associate Planner for the City of Reno. I found a two-acre plot of land out in the country, about 30 minutes from Reno. The idea of living in the country was appealing because it offered Lunar less opportunity to get in trouble or break her rehabilitation program. So, I bought the land and proceeded to build a house from a kit for the very first time. We lived together in a travel trailer for one year while I built the house.

While I was at work in Reno, Lunar would take my other car to Lake Tahoe, an hour's drive away, to meet her male friend. She told me about him and that he was an ex-convict, but really a nice guy. When I asked her if she was having an affair with him, she said no. I knew she was lying because I found her underwear in the hot tub, where they had been together.

One afternoon, she called to tell me she was taking the car to run off to Montana with him. I called the sheriff to report the car stolen. The highway patrol stopped them as they were about to enter Oregon. They were both arrested and put in jail in California for the possession of a stolen car. I had my car towed back. She called me from jail begging me to drop the charges. I tried to get the District Attorney to drop the charges, but I was told the State of California was pressing charges. The District Attorney really tried to give Lunar a chance for redemption, but Lunar failed to appear in court, which resulted in additional charges making her case now a felony. She ended up being sentenced to prison for one year.

While she was in prison, my life calmed down and I was experiencing peace for the first time in a very long time. I was pressing into God more and leaning on him more for clarity, balance and contentment.

Writing this chapter took an enormous amount of energy just to relive the drama. As I look back, I thank God for getting me through this and allowing me the opportunity to clean up my life. I am so thankful to have walked through the valley of darkness and despair to be able to share my life story. I hope my story will resonate with the misfortunate, the lost souls who have no hope, and that no matter what you've done, what you've been through, God can make a way.

This chapter represents the raw onions in my wish sandwich. Some people hate them, but I love them. Sometimes they make you cry, but they taste really good on a sandwich.

CHAPTER 9

A New Beginning

My new job as an Associate Planner for the City of Reno required me to present development plans to the Planning Commission and City Council. This new level of responsibility challenged me to up my game quite a bit as a professional planner. I had to learn how to write staff reports in a technical way that was clear and comprehensive to Council members that may not be well versed in the planning industry. On days that I presented projects to the Council, I would appear before them in a suit and tie and be prepared to answer any questions they had about the development projects.

One day, as I was preparing to present to the Council that evening, I was waiting in the lobby for the elevator when two ladies approached me. I recognized one of the ladies as the graphic designer that worked downstairs in the printing department. I had never met or seen the other lady. I learned she was also a graphic designer for the City of Reno and that her name was Michelle. She was an attractive blonde, very friendly, and had a nice smile.

Over the next two weeks, Michelle and I kept randomly bumping into each other in the lobby. We would smile at each other and say, "Hey, how's it going?" As these encounters kept happening, I would make the comment, "We should go grab lunch some time." She replied with a smile saying, "Name the place and time." We would both go about our business.

I was working in my office one morning when I heard a friendly voice say, "So this is where you hang out." I turned to look and there stood Michelle, smiling at me. I instantly jumped to my feet and said, "Oh hey, how's it going? What are you doing up here?" She replied, "I'm working on a project for your department and need to collect photos of employees. Can you come down to my office for a photoshoot later today?" "Sure!" I responded. Just then she noticed some of the photographs I had on my shelf. She pointed to one of the photos and said, "Who's this?" I immediately responded, "You don't know who this is?!" She looked at me with surprise and said, "No, who is it?" I smiled, and proudly said, "That's me with the legendary B.B. King. He is one of the most famous blues musicians there is!" "Oh," she replied, "Why are you in the photo with him?" Again, I smiled and explained, "Because my band opened for him when I lived in California." "Oh," she paused, "So, you're a musician?" "Yes!" I excitedly replied. "I'm a singer. My band was quite popular." She tilted her head and looked at me with renewed curiosity and remarked, "Huh! Very interesting." Her eyes seemed to smile at me. There was something special about this girl.

An hour or so later, I went down to Michelle's office to get my picture taken. During the photoshoot, I started asking her questions, because I wanted to know a little bit more about her. She shared with me that she was recently widowed, and that she had two young daughters. She seemed kind, and very genuine, and I was intrigued by her. I asked her if she would take me up on that lunch invite, and she said with a smile, "Yes. I'd like that."

Now that Michelle mentioned that her husband passed away, I remember hearing about a City of Reno employee that was gravely ill through the City's intranet. I didn't put the pieces together until I learned that it was Michelle's husband, who was a City engineer, who the messages were about. I felt so bad for her and her family.

We met at Applebee's. I was excited and nervous at the same time, because I liked her and didn't want to say something stupid that would blow it. We talked and laughed and connected very easily. We ended up having a lot of things in common. I couldn't stop smiling...or sweating. I was so nervous. Sweat kept pouring down from my bald head. I blamed it on the heat, but I sensed that she knew I was nervous too.

After work on Friday, I approached her in the parking lot as she was heading home. I asked her if she would like to go roller blading with me over the weekend. She smiled and said, "Well, that's something that I've never been invited to do before." She went on to explain that she had promised herself that she would finish painting her bedroom in the new house that she and her girls had just moved into. She invited me to come over to her house to help her paint if I wanted to hang out. I gladly accepted her invitation.

I thought I was a pretty good painter, but she ended up showing me how to sponge paint for effect and texture. She was creating an ocean room effect, and sponge painting turned out to be more time consuming than just rolling or brushing. It was enjoyable though, working alongside her and getting to know her. We ended up listening to oldies music while we painted. I was quite turned on to find out she liked oldies, because that was my genre. I learned that Michelle was 20 years younger than me, and she loved to sing too. We thoroughly enjoyed singing and harmonizing along with the oldies songs playing on the radio. It was the most fun I've ever had painting.

As our friendship grew, we would join each other for a walk during our morning and afternoon breaks. We often would sing praise songs during our walks and she would complement me on my harmonies. I loved the way she looked at life. She opened my eyes to see and appreciate things differently. She was full of vitality and loved to explore. We went to museums, had picnics in the park, danced, laughed, and talked for hours over the phone. I was infatuated.

I've always struggled with my weight, and I felt it was time to start focusing on improving my health. I went in for lapband surgery where they constrict the lower portion of my stomach with a band to reduce the amount of food it takes to make me feel full. It was an out-patient procedure and I was told to take it easy for the next couple of weeks.

Michelle and I had previously made plans to take her girls, ages 11 and 9, to visit Santa Cruz Beach and Boardwalk, in California, for the weekend. It was a five-hour drive from Reno. I didn't want my lap-band surgery to put a damper on our plans, so I agreed to join them as promised. The doctor said the only restrictions I had from my surgery was to eat a liquid diet for a few days. The Boardwalk is like a mini amusement park, with carnival-type rides and games you can play to win stuffed animals.

Being a big kid at heart, I opted to join them on one of the smaller roller coaster rides, because it didn't look too scary, and it didn't make you go upside down at all. It didn't take long for me to realize I made a huge mistake. After the first drop on the ride, I started screaming, "Make it stop! Make it stop! Oh God, make it stop!" Michelle laughed and laughed at me. She warned me not get on the ride, and here I was screaming, "Make it stop!" when we all knew there was no way we could make the ride stop until it was over. I've never been so happy to get off a ride in my life!

On our drive back from the boardwalk, we both decided it would be great to show the girls a bit of San Francisco. I had fallen in love with San Francisco when I previously experienced it before going to Vietnam. It was getting dark and we agreed it would be best to get a room for the night and explore the city and the zoo the next day. We got a hotel room with two queen beds and Michelle told the girls they can sleep together in one of the beds, and that she and I would share the other bed. This was my first opportunity to spend an intimate moment with Michelle. I was really starting to have strong feelings for her. I wanted the girls feel comfortable with our sleeping arrangements, so I put on my sleep apnea mask, which keeps me from snoring, and pretended to be a monster. They laughed and smiled and told me I was silly.

That night I was in heaven sleeping next to the most extraordinary women I had ever met.

Back at work the following week, I built up the courage to ask Michelle if she would be my girlfriend. She hesitated and then finally replied, "Sure." She had previously schooled me that dating should only happen if you plan to spend your life with that person. Honestly, I saw it a little differently. I felt dating could be the beginning of a long-term relationship, but not necessarily a commitment to marry. I went home that day after she agreed to be my girlfriend, and really began to do some soul searching. I came to the conclusion that I wasn't really ready for a dating commitment at that level. I also knew that if I didn't handle this dating relationship properly, a break-up could have everlasting damage to our friendship. I loved Michelle, and I didn't want to take advantage of her. I knew she was an exceptional woman and she deserved to be highly respected. When we went for our walk the following day, I said to her, "Maybe we should take it slow and not be a couple yet." I think she also had reservations because she quickly replied, "Okay."

So, we were back to being best friends. We went on many more adventures together that summer. We enjoyed camping up in the mountains, and even took the girls to Yosemite National Park along with a group of friends. We started making plans to visit New York City during Christmas and New Year's. I loved the idea of showing her around my hometown. There is a lot of cultural beauty and performing art productions in New York City that I knew would impress Michelle. She told me she would feel safer having a man with them while exploring the city.

Sometime later that summer, Michelle mentioned to me that she thought she should start dating again. She hadn't dated since she was 16 years old when she met her husband. She thought it would be good for her to go through the dating process and see what it brings about. I was mortified! I didn't want to lose my best friend. I told her, "You ain't gonna meet anybody better than me." She smiled and went on to tell me that I will always be her best friend, even if she has a boyfriend. She joined a dating service that set her up with possible matches during the lunch hour. After the date, she would share with me how it went while we walked on our break that afternoon. It was kind of entertaining to hear the stories, and learn about the various guys she met.

I knew deep down she wouldn't find anyone who loved her as much as I did. The search went on and on. One day the unthinkable happened. Michelle didn't show up for our afternoon walk and she didn't call, like we would usually do if one of us was going to be late or absent. As I was leaving the building, I saw Michelle in the parking lot. She was glowing like a bright light bulb and so happy. I said, "What's going on with you looking so happy?" She went on to explain that she met a really wonderful man at lunch, and she felt very good that it could turn into something real. I was happy for her, but I was also deflated.

In the coming weeks, I met her new boyfriend and tried to be very happy for both of them. Michelle and I still continued to take our break walks together and it was obvious her boyfriend didn't approve. He was a police officer and wanted to be the main man in her life. Michelle told him that she and I were only friends and nothing would ever change that. After dating for only three months, he proposed to her and she shockingly said, "Yes." I was devastated. The woman that I loved was never going to be with me the way I wanted to be with her.

I did my best to be the best friend she needed me to be. On one of our walks, Michelle mentioned that her fiancé wanted to go to New York with us. I said, "No," because that was our special trip. She and I planned it all out before he came into the picture. Having him there with us would change the entire dynamic. I was kind of hoping to use this trip to reignite some chemistry between Michelle and me. She emphasized that it would not be right for us to purposefully exclude her fiancé now that they were in a serious relationship. She was right, and I knew that either way, if he went with us or not, she was still his girlfriend.

Eight of us flew to the East Coast to explore New York: Michelle and her two daughters, her fiancé and his son, two other friends, and myself. We landed at Newark Airport in New Jersey just across the Hudson River from New York. Michelle's long-time friend and her daughter came down from Connecticut to explore New York with us as well. The plan was to stay at a hotel in New Jersey because the price of hotels in New York City was astronomical, especially during the holiday season. Michelle's fiancé began exuding his dominance as soon as we landed. He would make eye contact with me and then give Michelle a kiss on the lips while keeping one eye open to be sure I was looking at him with her. I wasn't liking it at all.

We rented a van and started driving toward Brooklyn to visit my sisters. Michelle and the others were experiencing culture shock. Newark is a predominately African-American city and it looked pretty run-down in some parts. There was a lot of graffiti, bars on windows, abandoned buildings, and trash everywhere. It was kind of unsettling for Michelle, who lived in Nevada her whole life. I, in turn, felt right at home.

We arrived at my sister's house and were warmly greeted by many family members I hadn't seen for years, and some that I had never met. Some of the ladies were busy in the kitchen cooking fried chicken and collard greens in preparation for the New Year's party. The air in the home was thick with the smell of chicken grease, so much so, that you could imaging scraping it off the wall. This was another moment of culture shock for Michelle and her girls. They were smiling and happy to be meeting my family members that they had only heard about.

My sister took me aside in the kitchen after introductions and asked me, "Who is that guy with Michelle? I thought you and her were together?" I said, "That is Michelle's fiancé. He's a policeman in Nevada." They remarked, "Whoa Buster, you better watch out for him. She has eyes for you, and he might just try to shoot you." I told them that I wasn't threatened by him, and that Michelle and I were just friends. They gave me a look that implied that they weren't convinced by what I just told them.

As night fell, my nephew, Smokey, offered to take us on a tour of Times Square in Manhattan. Since there were so many of us, we decided to take the subway. Ten of us walked two blocks down from my sister's house to the subway station in Brooklyn. While standing on the platform, waiting for the train, a young black man, dressed in dark clothes and wearing a red bandana walked onto the platform. Our diverse group of people definitely stood out from the locals, and we felt somewhat intimidated by the way this young man was looking at us. We had people in our group that were White, Black, Hispanic, Asian, American Indian, and of course there were children. Perhaps taking the subway from Brooklyn to Times Square wasn't the best choice, especially at night.

The young man approached our group with swagger and nodded his head at Smokey and said. "What's up Smoke. Who dis?" Smokey acknowledged him with an arm bump, a type of gangster handshake, and said, "This is my family, man." The young man nodded in acknowledgement and said. "Alright. Alright. That's cool." I was relieved to have Smokey with us because he was a big boy, about six foot, four inches, and 280 pounds. He was familiar with the territory, and I felt that my friends were safe under his watch.

As we walked the streets in Manhattan, I felt like a third wheel. Michelle's fiancé continued exuding his dominance by yelling at Michelle's daughters whenever he saw that they were hanging near me instead of being by his side. He seemed very intimidated by my presence. When we arrived back in Brooklyn after sightseeing, I told Michelle that I was going to spend some time with my family, and that I would meet up with them in a few days. I was saddened that our trip wasn't what I hoped it would be, but It was out of my control.

When we reunited a few days later I found out that things weren't going too well for Michelle and her fiancé on this trip either. They were bumping heads a lot, especially about her daughters and the way he treated them. By the time we boarded the plane back to Nevada things had gotten really testy between them; in fact, she sat next to me on the flight home. I am sure that probably pissed him off even more.

When we landed in Reno, my bags were missing. I had to go into the airline's missing luggage office to make my claim and arrange for later delivery to my home. Michelle was trying to help me file the claim when her fiancé insisted that she leave with him immediately. She said to him, "Let's just make sure Jerry gets everything taken care of before we leave him. It's late, and you don't just leave a friend behind if there's a way you can help." He was frustrated and tired, and said, "We're leaving." He grabbed his son and their bags and walked out of the airport, leaving Michelle and her girls with me. He didn't call her for weeks after that. I knew that wasn't going to sit well with her, because I didn't call her once when I should have, and she got super upset with me. Within a month after the trip to New York, they broke off their engagement. It was over. I felt bad for Michelle, but I didn't think he was right for her, so I was good with it.

Michelle and I continued to be best friends and enjoyed each other's company on a regular basis. Her extended family also embraced me as her best friend, and I really liked the way they made me feel as if I was part of their family. Michelle ended up meeting a gentleman at her church and they began dating. I thought he was a nice guy and maybe he would be the one for her. Although I still loved Michelle, it was different now. I knew I wasn't what she wanted.

Around that same time, I met a lady friend. She was really nice and she had a three-year-old boy. We were kind of feeling each other out to see if we had chemistry together. We dated for quite a few months, but I had my doubts about it turning into a long-term relationship. I wasn't into raising a three-year-old at my age.

Michelle invited us over to her house for an Easter celebration with her entire family. I remember feeling a little odd being at Michelle's house with another woman. It seemed as though Michelle may have felt it was odd too. Even though she was there with her new boyfriend, I caught her glancing over at me quite often and wondered what was going through her mind. I wanted her to be happy even if it meant that it wasn't with me.

She ended the relationship with her boyfriend shortly afterwards. During our lunch break, we walked around the park near our office as she vented. She went on and on about how hard it is to find a good man with quality character these days. I just listened, like a good friend would.

My vision was becoming a real issue at this point in my life and career. I was diagnosed with diabetic retinopathy and decided that driving long distances to and from work was not wise. I put my country home on the market to sell, and moved into my travel trailer at an RV park near my work.

My phone rang and it was Lunar. She was calling me from jail. She said she had no place to go, and she had been sober for a year. I begrudgingly allowed her to stay with me until she could get on her feet. I didn't tell Michelle about her staying with me because Michelle had previously mentioned that I shouldn't have let Lunar treat me badly, for as long as I did. I was sure Lunar would be gone within a few days anyway, so no need to upset Michelle with the details.

A couple of days later, at work during our morning walk, Michelle sensed that I was being a bit distant in my thoughts. She asked, "What's up with you?" I replied, "I got a lot on my mind." She asked, "Like what?" I commented, "An old friend has been staying with me the last couple of days, and it's throwing me off a bit." "Oh, yeah? Who's your friend?" she asked. I didn't want to lie, so I begrudgingly told her it was Lunar. Her lips tightened as she stared right into my eyes and said, "Oh! How long is she staying with you?" she asked. I told her, "I'm not sure but I think she'll be leaving soon. Last night she tried to get into bed with me and I was so repulsed that I kicked her out of the bed and told her to stay the hell away from me. She slept on the couch, but she was gone when I woke up this morning." Michelle just stared at me with her fists and lips tight. She didn't say anything else. She just walked away.

I felt it best to stay clear of Michelle while I dealt with the Lunar situation. I didn't want Lunar back in my life, but I wasn't about to see her homeless, either. I gave her one week to find a place to stay or I would drive her back up to Clearlake, California, where she could stay with family. She ended up finding a place to stay and I was so happy she was leaving. I really didn't want that negative drama in my life anymore.

Back at work a few days later, I got a call from Michelle telling me she wanted to talk with me. That made me a little anxious because I didn't know what to expect. We met in my car in the parking lot outside our office building. She began to tell me that she has stronger feelings for me than she originally thought. Evidently having Lunar enter my life again triggered something inside of Michelle. She went on to say that when she went on all of those lunch dates, she would end up comparing those men to me. She finally had come to the conclusion that she loved me as more than just a friend, because the idea of Lunar sleeping with me made her skin crawl, and she wanted to punch Lunar in the face multiple times.

I could not believe what I was hearing. My first impulse was, I didn't want to be heartbroken again, so I was somewhat apprehensive. I had worked hard to fall out love with Michelle in this way. She was still my best friend and I didn't want to lose that. I suggested we keep being friends for now, because her newfound feelings may change, and I was not sure if I was ready to open up my heart again.

This chapter represents the slices of juicy red tomatoes that add nutrients and flavor to my wish sandwich.

CHAPTER 10

Glory

A few weeks after the relationship conversation with Michelle, I received a call from Pennsylvania, where my dad was living. The call was from a cousin whom I had never met. She said, "Your father has had a stroke. He is in grave condition and he wants to see you." She put the phone to his ear and I said, "Daddy, hang on. I am catching the next flight out to be with you." He mumbled with excitement, and my cousin said his face lit up with joy when he heard my voice.

I immediately called my son and daughter to tell them the news about their grandpa. I then called Michelle to tell her that my father was gravely ill, and I needed to fly home to see him. I asked her, "Will you come with me to meet my dad? It would really mean a lot to me to have you there." After making some quick arrangements with her family and her boss, she said she could join me. I was so grateful to have her companionship. She had a way of calming me and making me feel that everything was going to be okay. Michelle, my son, and I flew out of Reno, Nevada, the next day and headed for JFK Airport in New York.

On the long flight across the country, I reminisced about my later adventures with my father....

My daddy and I had fostered a really good friendship throughout my adult years. When I lived in Denver, I would fly him out to Colorado to visit. Although he spent most of his life on the East Coast, I learned later that he loved to travel. So, I would fly him out west on several occasions. He was fascinated with all the mountains and vast lakes and open space. On occasion I took him on camping and fishing trips with me and his two grandchildren. I took him to Leadville, Colorado, and Turquoise Lake. It was about 10,000 feet in altitude with some of the best trout fishing in the world. The lake water was very cold, which was great for keeping my dad's beer cold. Fishing was good, so good that you couldn't get the catch off the line fast enough before you had another strike.

My dad told funny stories about life. He had a funny way of telling stories that made you laugh. We would exchange stories and just laugh and laugh. He told me that his barbecue was so good, that people would eat the bone. I said, "You must be joking right? Are you kidding me?" He said, "No, they asked for more sauce to go over the bone." That was just one of many funny stories he told.

My dad also found out that beer can be more intoxicating at higher altitudes. I had to help him back to the cabin and nurse him back from altitude sickness. My dad loved the outdoors just like me. He would stare at the majestic mountains and sky in a very appreciative and marveling way. I loved hanging out with my dad out west. Not so much on the East Coast, because he always seemed confrontational and agitated back east. I would prefer to fly him out west, as opposed to visiting him on the East Coast. When I moved to California, I flew him out to visit me and my kids. He loved it. I had a small motorboat. I took him for a joy ride on the lake.

When I moved to Nevada, I flew my dad out to visit me there too. He was probably in his late eighties then. I arrived at Reno/Tahoe Airport to pick him up. I was excited to see him and show him where I lived in Minden, Nevada, near Lake Tahoe. I met him as he walked out of the baggage claim terminal.

The very first thing I noticed was that he reeked of body odor and urine. Then as we walked toward the car he grabbed his crotch and said he had to pee. I asked, "Why did you walk by all the restrooms and not relieve yourself?" Before I could turn him around to take him to the bathroom, he was standing in a puddle of urine. I said, "You are not going to ride in the car with saturated pants and soil my seats." So, I found a thick blanket to put in the seat for him to sit on. He said, "Don't be mad, Son. I'm old and can't help myself." I said, "Dad, smelling like that is offensive to people, especially who sit next to you. They have remedies for that." I began to explain about adult underwear for people who have bladder control issues. He said, "I ain't wearing no diaper." I retorted, "You can't sit on my furniture, wetting yourself without it!" I insisted. So, we stopped at the pharmacy and purchased some adult underwear for him.

I got him home and helped him shower before putting the diaper on him. He absolutely loved it, and said he wanted to take some back home with him. I never saw my daddy naked before and most certainly never washed his body. I never knew he had such soft skin. Now I know where my soft skin came from.

My dad was so polite and well-mannered out west. He would greet everybody with, "Hello, how are you?" I took him to a casino, and he was very excited when he saw all that money. He would try to tilt the slot machines so he could win. I explained to him that was cheating, and they could throw him out of the casino. It was almost like we had reversed roles. I was now the adult in the room.

We landed at JFK and my son rented a car. We drove to Brooklyn and stayed the night at my oldest sister's house. The next day, we picked up my other sister and headed to Scranton, Pennsylvania, where my father was hospitalized. We walked into his room where my cousin met with us. This was my first time ever meeting her. She explained my father's condition was grave, and the doctors weren't sure how many days he had left.

We entered daddy's room, and he was lying still on the bed. I moved closer to his bedside and said, "Daddy, I'm here. I brought my son and my best friend who I want you to meet." He opened his eyes and excitedly mumbled while reaching his hand toward my face. We hugged. He was happy to see me. I introduced Michelle and he mumbled and smiled as he waved at her. We sat with him until visiting hours were over. My cousin offered us lodging in her home. She was a beautiful person who loved and cared for my daddy. Her father was my daddy's late brother. Out of 10 brothers and sisters, my dad was the last surviving sibling.

That evening, we all met at my cousin's for dinner and conversation, and to pay tribute to my father. Michelle was treated like a celebrity. It was a little unusual for a white woman from Nevada to be gathered amongst all these blacks in a predominately black community. She was easygoing and blended right in with my family. That was one of the many things I loved about Michelle, she was genuinely authentic, just loving people. My cousins and their friends fed us a delightful meal of collard greens, sweet potatoes, fried chicken, and peach cobbler pie. Michelle had never had collard greens before. This was a popular dish for black folks; we called it soul food. She must have enjoyed it because before you knew it, her plate was empty and she was asking for more.

My cousin gave Michelle and me a room to sleep in that only had one bed. I guess she assumed we were a couple, even though we were just best friends. I was so appreciative of Michelle being there with me at this time, because it was hard to see my dad in this fragile state. I knew he was going to die, and it was comforting having my best friend with me in this unfamiliar place. We embraced each other as we fell asleep.

The next day, my brother Pete arrived from Kentucky, where he lived with his girlfriend. I was excited to see Pete. I hadn't seen him for almost twenty years. We went to visit dad together. They had him heavily sedated. He was in and out of consciousness. We were told we should prepare to say goodbye because his condition was deteriorating fast. My brother Pete, my sister, my son, Michelle, and I all stood around my dad and sang, "Daddy's Home." The hospital staff and patients said we sounded so good they thought we were professionals. I kissed daddy on the forehead, as we all left the room.

We drove back to Brooklyn that night because my daughter was flying in from Dallas. I was sitting in the back seat with my sister, and my son was driving. My sister said, "Michelle I just knew you and Buster were meant to be together." She went on to say, "That last time you visited with that other guy, I knew something was off. I'm so glad to see you and Buster together."

Michelle turned and looked at me from the front passenger seat and replied, while smiling, "I don't know what you mean. Jerry and I are just friends, right Jerry?" She had that look in her eyes that made my heart flutter. I replied with a smile saying, "Uh, yeah. I guess so." I knew I was the one holding the cards. She had claimed her love for me back in Reno, and I was quickly realizing that I did indeed want to spend the rest of my life with this woman. I needed to make my move soon, but this wasn't the right time.

It was good to see my daughter again. This was the first time that she and Michelle were able to meet in person. They had spoken over the phone a few times, but it was delightful to see my two favorite women getting to know each other. The following morning, we loaded up in two cars and headed back to Pennsylvania to visit Daddy one last time. He had been unconscious and unresponsive for a couple of days now. The doctors said he was not expected to survive the night, and that he was comfortable and not in any pain. It was bitter-sweet to see him so vulnerable like that. Tough guy goes soft in the end. I'm very thankful that he and I were able to have a somewhat pleasant relationship as we both got older. He was my dad, and I loved him.

We spent our last few days in New York visiting family in Brooklyn and exploring the city. This was my opportunity to show Michelle the New York I grew up in. This was our New York trip that we didn't get to have because of her engagement to someone else on our last trip.

We always had fun when we were together. We both loved to laugh, be silly, and explore new places. We were walking down the streets in Harlem when we came upon a street vendor selling music DVDs. I grabbed Michelle's hand and together, we started doing the cha-cha on the sidewalk of 125th Street and Lenox Avenue. We saw the famous Apollo Theatre where big names like James Brown, The Temptations, Richard Pryor, and many other famous black artists had performed. We went into different clothing stores and tried on expensive outfits, pretending to be rich and famous. I walked into a store that sold wigs and braids for black people. I went up the counter and took my hat off, exposing my bald head and exclaimed, "Hook me up with some braids!" Michelle started laughing at my obvious silliness, but the clerks behind the counter just looked at me in disgust. We took a look around the store and I found a hat that had braids attached to it. I put it on and asked Michelle, "How do I look?" She giggled and said, "Whoa, you look like a whole new man!" She snapped my picture.

We boarded the subway and headed to the Bronx. On the subway, we would make googly eyes at each other, while pretending to be serious like everyone else around us. We couldn't help but crack a smile because of the faces we would make at each other. I took her to Yankee Stadium where the New York Yankees played professional baseball. A few blocks away was where Woodycrest Children's home used to be. I showed her the buildings, which were now converted into a mental hospital. I told her many stories of my childhood while living there. She couldn't believe how steep the street was where I would roller skate down, doing my best to avoid skating into heavy traffic at the bottom. She was intrigued and fascinated by everything that I was showing her.

As the evening hours approached, we ventured over to the City of Manhattan. We took the elevator up to the top of Rockefeller Center that stood in the town's center. From the Top of the Rock, we had a spectacular view of the entire city. Not too far away in the city skyline we could see the Empire State Building. From one side, we were able to see all of Central Park, and from another side, we could see across the Hudson River into New Jersey. The view was absolutely magnificent and only improved as night fell.

The city lights lit up the sky and we felt that we were in another world. It was mesmerizing. I wrapped my arms around Michelle and said to her, "Michelle, I've got something important to ask you." She looked at me with a smile and said, "What is it?" I replied, "Will you be my girlfriend?" She smiled and said, "Yes, on one condition." I instantly remarked, "What condition?" She then stated, "I will be your girlfriend if you promise to never have anything to do with Lunar, ever again." I quickly rebutted, "Lunar who?" Michelle smiled at my response and leaned in to give me a confirming kiss. We stayed up on the Top of the Rock for a while longer, kissing and embracing each other, taking in the richness of this blissful moment in time.

Michelle and I enjoyed dating one another for months before I decided to propose. Since we worked in the same building, I wanted to include some of our coworkers into the grand gesture, so that it was more impactful and impressive to Michelle. I didn't want to screw this up! I went to each floor of our building and asked my coworkers to come down to the print shop where Michelle worked at 2:00 p.m., because I was going to propose.

At 2:00 p.m., I came into Michelle's office with a big smile on my face. She turned around to see a bunch of people behind me, all smiling. She noticed how big I was smiling, and asked, "What is going on?" I got down on one knee, pulled out the ring and said, "Michelle, I've been loving you for a long time, and I want to take this moment to ask for your hand in marriage. Will you do me the honor of marrying me?" She replied with a smile and a resounding, "YES!" We kissed and hugged while our friends cheered.

We were married August 8, 2008. It was a beautiful, tropical-themed wedding held in an arboretum with waterfalls meandering throughout. After the wedding ceremony, everyone walked over to the reception hall. The interior of the hall was an atrium, landscaped with trees, shrubs, and coy-filled ponds located throughout. When Michelle and I entered the reception room, we were greeted with thunderous cheer and standing ovation. We walked around shaking hands and giving hugs. Being a musician, I was used to applause, but this recognition was different and overwhelmingly heartfelt. Family and friends were connecting, dancing, laughing, and having a memorable good time. I had the chance to perform one song with the live band. I sang "Mustang Sally" by Wilson Pickett. Everybody was cheering and dancing and smiling. It was the best party I had thrown in my life. I was so happy. I fell in love with an angel. Life was like a dream.

We flew to Jamaica for our honeymoon. We were escorted to our bungalow by our butler for the week, Kesmit. We had a beautiful view of the ocean from our private patio, and we had our own private pool. Our butler told us about our complimentary dining options and various excursions we could get scheduled. Once he learned that I was a singer, he highly recommended that I perform in the staff and guest talent show.

A few nights later into our honeymoon, Michelle and I made our way over to the amphitheater where the talent show was taking place. The place was packed. We found some seats near the floor, off to the side of the stage. I heard my name being called, so I rose up and took the stage. The Jamaican band seemed to have forgotten the intro to my song that we had briefly rehearsed earlier that day, so I did what any professional performer would do. I improvised.

The song I was attempting to sing was "Tell It Like It Is," by Aaron Neville. I began to ad-lib by engaging the audience with some questions. "Fellas, who out there loves their woman?" All the men roared. I went on to ask, "How many of you are here on your honeymoon?" The entire stadium erupted with cheer. I began to share, "Let me tell you about the woman I love." They cheered as I walked over to where Michelle was sitting. I got down on one knee in front of her as the audience stood to their feet and cheered even louder. I reached for Michelle's hand and said, "Baby, I just love you so much. You mean the world to me. Thank you for marrying me." Michelle blushed bright red as the crowd continued to whistle and cheer.

I stood up from my kneeling position, just as I heard the band finally land their note, and began singing, "Tell It Like It Is." My rich vocal tone washed over the crowd and women began to swoon in ecstasy. As I finished my performance, the crowd roared to their feet and began chanting, "Jerry! Jerry! Jerry!"

This Chapter represents the spice of life. The ultimate ingredient for a rich, nourishing, and satisfying life sandwich. OMG that is good!

NOW IT'S YOUR TURN

The poor black boy from Brooklyn has completed his journey. His sandwich is complete. From Ghetto to Glory.

What about you? What ingredients are you choosing from life to include in your wish sandwich?

Whether you believe it or not, your circumstances do not, and should not define your destiny. You always have choices. Sometimes you just need help finding the open door. This is where a mentor comes in handy. These are people who have been where you are, and have navigated their way to where you want to be. You might be thinking this is easier said than done. Well, let me tell you from my life experience, it is a matter of mindset and determination.

You may have heard the saying, "You can do it, if you put your mind to it." First you must believe that change is possible. Then you must authentically want change to take place. Without belief and desire, you will not be motivated to do the work it takes to bring about the change you seek.

Learning should never stop. I'm still challenged to stay informed and current in my industry so I can lead my company to success. Every day I am committed to show up to work. I trust that God will lead me, and I do what I need to do. No excuses. Addictions can be overcome. Circumstances can be changed. It's your choice.

By: Jerry B. Bowden (Buster)

Peace, love and prosperity!

Remember in life you have choices, which will you choose!

IN MEMORY

Mathew Sam Bowden, My Father

Mary Magdalene Bowden, My Mother

Johnny Raymond Bowden, My Brother

Wendell Bowden, My Brother

While writing this book, my brother Butch (Wendell) passed away in March 2018. Wendell Bowden was 70 years old. He was a Vietnam Veteran war hero and served as a U.S. Army Medic.

As you know from reading this story, we were close in age, and were together most of the time growing up, not necessarily by choice. Nevertheless, my brother was, despite our differences, my friend and I regret not showing him more love. Rest in peace, Wendell. God be with you!

ABOUT THE AUTHOR

Born in Brooklyn, New York, Jerry Bowden joined the U.S. Army in 1966, at age 17, to escape poverty, violence, and despair. After serving in South Korea and Vietnam, he was discharged from military service in 1971.

Jerry was married in 1970 and has two adult children who now have families and careers of their own.

Mr. Bowden started attending community college in 1975, and graduated with a Master's Degree from the University of Colorado College of Planning and Design In 1986.

He unfortunately contracted diabetic retinopathy, along with other health complications, from his service in Vietnam. His diminished vision resulted in disability retirement in 2011 from city government.

Jerry and his new wife, Michelle Calloway Bowden, started a tech company in 2016, which focused on augmented reality interactive marketing campaigns. Jerry is the President of Revealio - Software and Media Solutions, located in the San Francisco Bay Area. Follow him on LinkedIn and Facebook.

ENDORSEMENT

"Success comes in cans, not cannots. Jerry B. Bowden is living proof of what a 'can do' attitude is able to overcome and achieve in life. His powerful story of transition from ghetto to glory is beyond inspirational for anyone wishing to experience their fullest potential, regardless of their circumstances. Throughout this book, you will be jolted, awakened, and moved. You will experience adventure, despair, and fame. Jerry B. Bowden pulls you into his world through colorful storytelling, in this true-to-life novel of a poor black boy overcoming tremendous adversity, to step into a life of abundance and success."

—Joel Weldon, President
Hall of Fame professional speaker
Creator of the Ultimate Speaking System
www.ultimatespeaker.com

REVIEWS

"Jerry takes you on a journey of his life and into his mindset of how he has consistently overcome adversity. Wish Sandwich will open your mind to the possibilities that surround you and begin to see your life from a new perspective."
   —September Dohrmann, CEO of CEO Space International
www.ceospaceinternational.com

"I've always said, 'you will know what a person is made of when they are challenged in life, and you see what spills out of their life.' *Wish Sandwich* reveals a journey of how a person was made through hardships, difficulty, disappointment, and perplexities, but yet by God's design has triumphed. It truly expresses the old adage, 'it's not where you start, or even the journey along the way, but how you persevere and never give up on yourself.' My hope is as you read this book, you will be encouraged to never give up."
   —Nathan DuPree
Pastor, Living Stones Church
www.livingstoneschurches.com

"Within the pages of this book, you will find many universal truths. Jerry B. Bowden has captured a really powerful life in a powerful way that made this book very easy to read and relate to. A story of heartache, family violence, redemption, poverty, and homelessness, Jerry's story is one of many African Americans from every era. A story of service, rebuilding and redesigning one's future, his saga will undoubtedly inspire others to aim higher. A story of personal struggle, excess, darkness and light, Jerry leaves the readers with tangible proof that the redemption songs within our souls are greater than the songs we sing in nightclubs or at unsafe workplaces, wishing for a life worth remembering. This is the American dream!"

—Leigh Bursey, Co-Author of *Bloom and Shine*, Columnist for *Invisible People*, International Chartered Housing professional, musician, motivational speaker, formerly homeless youth.
leighbursey@gmail.com

"Mr. Jerry B. Bowden is a natural storyteller. Wish Sandwich is vivid, moving and immersive to captivate and transport the reader deep in fiction-like struggles from the ghetto and war zone jungle to success and true love. Serious readers will learn the transformative power of fully embracing and experiencing life even in hardships where golden nuggets called blessings are hidden. I highly recommend Wish Sandwich to anyone in need of inspiration for their own personal battles."

—Fabien W. Edjou, Life Coach | Author | Blogger
www.revelationsandwonders.com

"In *Wish Sandwich*, Jerry shines a bright light on the dark tyranny of racism, childhood neglect, and addiction. Rather than succumbing to the charms of these devious seducers, he passionately sought the redemptive qualities of enlightenment, experience, and expressive prayer. Tucked within the pages of this engaging read are numerous recollections of a man fighting to lay claim to his God-given right to live a life free from binds and constraints. Jerry's emergence from the depths of suppression and bondage is nothing short of inspiring. One cannot help but become transformed by this hero's journey. Treat yourself and those you love to a satisfying Wish Sandwich today!"

—Tesy Ward
Foundress and CEO of The Tesy Ward Organization
www.TesyWard.com

Wish Sandwich is the epic story of Jerry Bowden's triumph in the face of overwhelming adversity. After being raised in mind-numbing poverty in Brooklyn, Jerry carried into his turbulent early adulthood the scars of a violently abusive father, a broken family, and years in the foster care system.

Yet, this is a magnificent story of overcoming. Eventually, Jerry faced down the demons that ran rampant in his life. With God's help, Jerry eventually earned a master's degree, established a successful career in public service, and has enjoyed a fulfilling Christ-centered marriage for many years. *Wish Sandwich* is a vivid reminder that, with God's grace, anything is possible!"

—Steve Bond, Lead Pastor, Summit Christian Church

"*Wish Sandwich* is full of action-adventure and suspense! Jerry B. Bowden shares his life's journey through such colorful storytelling that I felt like I was in the story with him. I was on the edge of my seat throughout the book, in suspense, wondering how he was going to get out of a harrowing situation, or where his escapades would take him next.

I felt his exhilaration playing dangerously as a child, his fear in a Vietnamese war zone, and his desire to win over the woman of his dreams. From the ghetto to the jungle, I was really struck by how Jerry always took pleasure in finding life enjoyable, even when his circumstances seemed awful.

Although Jerry made mistakes along his way, God intervened multiple times when he nearly died, and used his life events to mold him into the more mature, godly man he is today. I love that his desire is to encourage others to further themselves with education, and to make the right choices towards a fulfilling, godly life, while realizing that no one is limited by his or her circumstances.

In writing memoirs, it is sometimes difficult to convey your thoughts and memories in a meaningful way to others. Jerry's exposé does just that, and *Wish Sandwich* is a must read for anybody going through a tough time. You will be glad you did."

—Shiela Miller, Author, *Memoirs of a Miracle Baby, A Testimony of God's Love*
www.shielamiller.com

"The narration of *Wish Sandwich* was colorfully constructed in such a way that I could hear the author's voice in each word. As each life experience was orated, the detail and imagery made it easy to envision the environment and the emotion connected to each story.
This is a book that many men, especially African-American men, can relate to as it speaks to the daily struggles of life and how one can overcome them. I found myself wanting to hear more of the moments of victory to feel connected with the triumphant parts of this robust life story."
—Pastor Warnell Brooks, MFT, Worship & Pastoral Care, The Bay Church

"*Wish Sandwich* is a compelling story of rising above your circumstances, using your God-given gifts and talents, and the opportunities life presents you to achieve what you desire. Jerry B. Bowden, does an amazing job at, not only sharing his story but explaining how the feelings, emotions, and hardships in life can transform you from Ghetto to Glory if you choose to let them. I love his transparency, I could feel the resilience and determination, in every chapter. I believe Jerry's story of building a Wish Sandwich is very timely and relevant for the times we live in and will change the lives of its readers."
—Dr. Elizabeth Clamon CEO, founder of The Clamon Group, LLC, Award-winning international speaker and author, Expert Storytelling and Business Growth Strategy Coach
www.ElizabethClamon.com

"*Wish Sandwich* takes the reader through an impactful life story, probing and motivating the reader towards the realization that it is choices we make and not the circumstances we are dealt with that determine our success."
—Dr. Kasthuri Henry, PhD, CTP. CEO, KasHenry Inc | #1 International Best-Selling Author | Professor
www.kashenry.com

Made in the USA
Las Vegas, NV
31 December 2020